This One's Just 4 U

Sharon Barbee Simmons

SHARON BARBEE SIMMONS

Acknowledgment

Thanks be to God for the fruition of a dream deferred. He remains forever faithful.

Thank you to my late husband William "Billy Bob" Simmons who for years encouraged me to write a book. He always saw me putting my pen to the paper but never got to see the finished product. I love and miss you.

To all my sons, daughters, daughters-in-law, granddaughters and grandsons who always had faith that I could do this even when I didn't think I could, thank you for believing in me.

To the people who read some of my work and felt inspired, encouraged and sometimes shocked by it, thank you. You too, made it easier for me to stop procrastinating.

It takes a village- Thank you, village.

Preface

This book is a freestyle and unorthodox collection of poems, stories, and thoughts. It is with my sincerest aspiration that within the covers of this book you will find you- your faith- your hope- your truth- your fear- your victory- your healing- your strength- your courage and answers that are just for you.

So, please just pick a page and begin your journey into what-who and where you see yourself as being. If after finding you, you realize you have found someone else, please share.

Written with great hope and expectation. Enjoy your read!

Sharon Barbee Simmons

THIS ONE'S JUST 4 U

PICK A PAGE

SHARON BARBEE SIMMONS

NOT PERFECT

I have no stones to throw at anyone else

My house is glass and easily broken

I judge no one else, for I want no one to judge me

In me there is no perfection

For I am not perfect

I am only forgiven

Reflections

_____

_____

DON'T STOP

If our God was a

Tit for a Tat God

We would all be tatted up by now

It would be game over

For all of us, not just you

Keep Coming - Keep Moving

It ain't over - Don't Stop

Reflections

_____

_____

NEVER GIVE UP

Thank You, God, for breathing Your breath into me one more time

If there is breath - there is life

If there is life - there is hope

If there is hope.......

The possibilities are endless

Never give up!

Reflections

_____

_____

SECRETS

Did you grow up in a generation that had a "Whatever goes on in this house stays in this house" mentality? I did.

It was just the norm. I never knew anything else. No transparency. Transparencies- what was that?

That term was not even a part of our everyday vocabulary until, I would say, a few years ago with all the Trevon Martins, George Floyds, Freddie Grays, Brianna Taylors, Mike Browns, Tamir Rices, Ahmaud Arberys that we have encountered, and the list continues.

But these are not the kind of transparencies - secrets that I am talking about.

I am talking about the family secrets that can alter your life and change everything you believed in your heart to be true.

Titles given to people to whom they didn't belong: Mamas really Aunties - Aunties really Mamas - Uncles really Fathers – Fathers were just a one-night stand - Sisters not Sisters - Brothers not Brothers - Sisters really Cousins - Cousins really Brothers, and any other combination of relations that you may imagine.

Shared bloodline in some that you thought not

No bloodline in some you were sure about

There were hidden second families - divorces – domestic abuse – marriages - adoptions - births – adulteries that only a chosen few knew existed.

Wow! My head is spinning, and I can't comprehend how I kept all this stuff – all these lies locked up within.

9

It has been years – a generation has passed. I still haven't let all these things go – haven't let it out.

Now my children are finding out – blaming me – accusing me – judging me. Not understanding that no matter how unacceptable it seems to them – I never thought I had a choice.

That was how I was trained – how I was taught. We all were.

I did the best I could with what I had. We all did.

"Don't make waves." "If it ain't broke, don't fix it." "Let sleeping dogs lie." These were the proverbs that that I lived by. We all did.

Today, my children are being transparent with their children to the point of hurt – to the point of pain.

Do you think that maybe that was what I was trying to avoid – the hurt – the pain? Maybe that was what we were all trying to do back then.

They are not keeping secrets anymore. They are letting everything out. They are telling all they know - the good – the bad – the ugly. Nothing is being held back – no questions asked that are not answered without the complete truth.

Even though I find myself in an embarrassment zone, I am elated that they are demanding to know the truth – wanting to know the truth – needing to know the truth.

They are holding me (us) accountable to be the "Truth Bearers" in their lives so that they are able to become the "Truth Bearers" in the lives of the next generation and every future generation thereafter.

There will be no more secrets – there will be no more lies.

If it happens – we tell it

THIS ONE'S JUST 4 U

If it hurts – we bare it

I am (we are) now the first generation of the

"TRUTH BEARERS"

NO MORE SECRETS

Reflections

_____

_____

THE LIFTER

Let The Lifter of your head lift it high. High enough to see the Son even amid the rain and the storm that is trying to discourage you.

You can trust The Lifter to lift your head high enough for your eyes to see the hills from which cometh your help and to know that He that keepeth Israel and you never slumbers nor sleeps.

What does that mean to you? It means The Lifters got you, and He is aware of all you are going through because He is always with you – always able to lift you to the rock that is higher than you. The rock that gives you a clear view above the rain and storms of life that are trying to overtake you in this present place – at this present time.

Reflections

_____

_____

"NO"

Some of God's "No's" have saved your life, and twenty years later, you are still saying, "Thank You, God."

Reflections

_____

_____

BE STILL

When in the quietness – the stillness of the moment, you know that you have done all you can possibly do, be still. Be still and know that God is God.

Reflections

_____

_____

JUST PRAY

Right now, I just don't feel like talking. Right now, there are no words for you to say to me. I am in this place where nothing makes sense, and my mind is trying to catch up to where my spirit is trying to be.

But, for now, please, no words. Just your presence with no demands on me is all I need. Sit for a while and silently pray that your friend will soon be okay.

Reflections

_____

_____

WHEN I DON'T KNOW

No one knows

How my heart feels – how my head feels – how my soul feels

When I don't know

When I don't know where you are or if you are okay

When I don't know if you are with people who love you like I do
or with people who just don't care

People who will encourage you to do wrong, and at times, you
may encourage them, too. People –homies –friends who you trust
and depend on but will leave you at the drop of a hat

They won't know what happened to you or how you got that way
when something bad happens

Friends who will leave you beside a road – in a house – in a car, or
at a door because answering questions about you would surely be
too much of a threat to them – their safety – their freedom

No one knows how my heart feels – how my head feels – how my
soul feels

When I don't know

When I don't know when you walk out that door where you go
When I don't know if I will ever see you again

When every time the phone rings, I struggle whether to answer it
or not. Yes or No?

Yes, because I must know – I must know if my child has gone to
that place I prayed they would never go before me

No one knows how my heart feels – how my head feels – how my soul feels

When I don't know

When one more time God has spared your life – allowed you to do your own thing once more

Don't be deceived – don't feel untouchable or invisible.

Man may not be able to get you any time he pleases, but you are always right there for God's picking- His timing- His purpose – His plan

You are not your own. You have been bought with a price, and sooner or later, the bill will become due. Money can't pay it only your heart and soul will do. There will be no hiding place for you

Well, you can come easy, or you can come hard - that choice is up to you. Just be assured that you will come.

Reflections

_____

_____

IT WILL GET BETTER

I realize how hard it is for you to accept that bad things don't only
happen to other people

But they also happen to you

I am so very sorry for what you are going through right now

It will get better

Reflections

_____

_____

YET YOU LOVE ME

My heart says, "Thank you." Thank You, God, for loving me. Why You do, Lord, I don't know.

I have failed You so many times – let You down more than I can count or care to say.

Yet, You love me.

I cannot tell You in words – cannot exactly say how I feel. I know, though, that You already know.

I have somehow grown farther away from You than I ever thought I could – ever thought I would.

Yet, You love me.

For so long, I was so strong. My strength is gone now, and I hurt. I hurt because I miss being in communion with You. Still, I do nothing to change that.

Yet, you love me.

Tears well up in my eyes when I think of all that I have lost in my relationship with You.

I used to lie in Your arms and feel you rock all my fears and cares away. I don't do that anymore.

Yet, you love me.

Reading Your word used to bring me such revelation. Now, I sometimes find it hard to understand.

Yet, you love me.

Get back on track. Get back on track. I know that is what I need to do. Why can't I? It's easy, right? You get off, you get back on. I don't seem to be able to do that.

Yet, you love me.

My soul is crying out to You – my mind does not hear. I am in here somewhere. Though, at times, I may seem lost. I must not stop trying to get back to that place in You where I belong.

Every day I must strive harder than I did the day before. I cannot lose. This is a fight I cannot give up - too much is at stake.

No matter how hard it gets or how pointless it may seem, I must get back to You-I must not forget that You love me and that I do love You

Reflections

_____

_____

GAME CHANGER

When everyone thought that they knew, because of the life I was living, what the end would be for me

They bet against me, not knowing that when they bet against me, they were actually betting against YOU, and YOU,

YOU never lose

With one drop of Your blood

One touch of Your hand

One word from Your mouth

You changed the outcome of the game

You're a game changer

Nothing about me will ever be the same

Reflections

_____

_____

JUST FOR YOU

My prayer for you as you go through this difficult time is that God will surround you with His presence and His love.

That even now, you can be assured that God Knows - He Sees - He Hears, and He Is always with you.

Reflections

_____

_____

DON'T FORGET

"I don't need you for nothing."

"I am so glad that you don't.

Just don't forget there was a time you did."

Reflections

_____

_____

SEE

I struggle to see myself as You see me

Make me know that only the way You see me matters

Reflections

_____

_____

REASONS

I have given God a million reasons not to love me

None of them have changed His mind

Reflections

_____

_____

SHARON BARBEE SIMMONS

I SAW NOTHING

I saw nothing in me, God, that you could want

I saw nothing in me that you could love

I saw nothing in me for you to care about

Yet, you saw something and chose me anyway

You told me to follow You

When I could see nothing but blackness because of the sinful life I
lived

You saw inside the blackness because you are THE LIGHT

You called my name - reached inside and took me out

You let me see the light that was You

You told me that if I followed You - I could forever leave the
darkness behind

I could forever be with You in the light that is You

How You must have loved me, because I did not choose You -
You chose me - You loved me first

I could not even see You for all the blackness that surrounded me

To You there was no blackness - Everything was the same

You saw through it all

There is no place for sin to hide from You

There is no place for Your people to hide from You

Your light overcomes the dark and shines in every place

Darkness cannot comprehend it, nor can it comprehend You

Thank You for the Light that shone on me

Thank You for loving me then - now and always

Reflections

_____

_____

YOU REMEMBER

I never have to remind You not to forget about me, for I am always
on Your mind

You know all that I have need of today

Reflections

_____

_____

BEST LAID PLANS

Whatever your plans may be,

remember God has His own

Reflections

TAKE CARE OF YOU

Don't want to be so involved in someone else's life

that you fail to take thought of your own

Reflections

_____

_____

NOT TOO MUCH FOR GOD

There is nothing so wrong with you that God cannot fix

His arms are not too short that He cannot save

His ear is not so heavy that He cannot hear

His eyes are always in all places

Talk to the God that sees and hears you

Reflections

_____

_____

I CAN'T HEAR YOU

"My word is My voice. When you read My word, I am talking to you.

Anytime you want to hear from Me, go to My word."

Reflections

_____

_____

YOU THINK?

If we're going to say, "Lord, forgive me for saying this, but."

Maybe it is something we shouldn't say

You think?

Reflections

_____

_____

LOVE YOURSELF

Feeling lonely? You don't have to feel that way.

Do as I do; I thank God for allowing me to love myself enough to enjoy my own company.

You know what? I like me.

Start speaking to yourself, "I like me, and I enjoy my own company."

Speak it and believe it.

Reflections

_____

_____

INSTEAD

Instead of me, it was You

Instead of me getting what I deserved, it was You

Instead of me suffering the pain, it was You

Instead of me dying, it was You

Thank You, for You

Reflections

_____

_____

MY HUSBAND

What is a husband? A husband is one who will love his wife

as Christ loved the church and gave himself for it.

You, husband, have loved me not only as you love yourself,

but far more love have you given to me.

You have loved me for many years, since the days of our youth.

I have changed. My hair is a little gray,

and my hourglass figure has surely gone away.

Wrinkles are now appearing on my face,

and of that first girl you loved, sometimes I cannot find a trace,

but you seem to always find her.

You find her when she cannot find herself.

You are there when she knows not where she herself is.

You go to God on her behalf when she is sick- tired – lost - weary
and cannot find her way.

You are forever lifting her before the Lord.

Years ago, you promised to love me in good times and bad. God
knows we have had these times, yet you have remained strong for
us.

In sickness and in health and as surely as we have lived, these
things have come into our lives and may continue to come.

For richer poorer, we have been in both of these places
throughout our lives, but we have always been rich in God. The

wisdom He has bestowed on you, no amount of money could buy. I love you for the wisdom you possess.

Until death do us part, I again make a vow to you, my husband, that whatever comes or goes, I am determined to stand by you - to never leave you out - to never make you ashamed and to always remember what a blessing from God you are to me.

I will continue to pray that our daughters will seek holy men like their father - that our sons will lead their families with love as you have and that we will all continue to follow you as you follow Christ.

Be encouraged my husband, for you are highly favored by God and greatly loved by me. I give you all the love one woman can have for one man – my man - you. I give you me - a daughter of your Lord and Saviour Jesus Christ - the mother of your children and the love of your life always and forever.

HAPPY ANNIVERSARY!

Reflections

_____

_____

YOU

"You ain't never gonna be nothin'. You are just like your no-good daddy and your tramp of a mama. You ain't never gonna have nothin'. Your daddy was a drunk. You gonna be drunk. Your mama was stupid. You stupid - you lazy - you fat - you ugly- you skinny – you ignorant."

What child, what adult could survive hearing these words every day? Words that tear your soul to pieces - that attack every bit of self-worth you even thought you had.

Words that brought so many tears to your eyes that you can no longer cry. You feel numb - numb to the point of your mind telling you that you have no use - no one cares about you - you are a mess up - a screw-up. Nothing is ever going to change for you, not for the better at least, so why not put yourself out of this miserable thing called life? Take some pills - shoot yourself - cut your wrist - drive off a bridge - jump. YES, do that! Any one of those will do.

"No, don't do that." the small voice of God whispers to you. You hear it. It didn't sound like that loud "Yes, do that." you heard a few minutes ago.

This voice was calm-soothing and caring. He was telling you that He has already given His life for you because He loved you from the beginning - He loves you now - He will always love you. He is replacing all the negativity that has ever been told to you by anyone, including you.

You see, He has a plan for your life. You are enough, just like you are. You are fearfully and wonderfully made. He is the one that fashioned you. You are beautiful and smart. He has put so many gifts and ideas inside of you that have not even been tapped. You have not even begun to see who you are or what you are going to become when you put yourself in the Master's hands.

No doubt you are hurting, and the hurt is real. He is the one that can take that hurt away - fix every broken part of you and fill all the holes in your soul. He can renew your mind and erase every negative thought that has ever been planted. He can give you a new heart so that you can love without fear of consequences.

So, lift your head. Let the tears flow. Tears of hope - new promises of a new life. A new life in the One who gave His life to make all of this newness possible.

Say to yourself, "I shall not die but live and declare the works of the Lord."

Life is worth living.

Reflections

_____

_____

SHARON BARBEE SIMMONS

YOURS

As mixed up and messed up as I might be,

I am yours, God

Even on my worst day, I am still yours

Reflections

I'M TIRED AREN'T YOU

Can't we get past our past –check every bad thought at the door, and come together before it is too late?

Our lives are not getting longer. They are getting shorter moment by moment - hour by hour -day by day.

Can't we admit that we both bear the burden for how all of this has played out?

I am tired. Aren't you?

It takes too much energy to blame - to hate- to always be on guard in a fight or flight mode. I don't want to do this anymore.

Every encounter or conversation between us at some point goes totally left even though that was not the intention – Hollering - screaming - cursing, and saying things that we don't really mean. How can we mean these words that we spew at each other and STILL say that we love God?

I'm tired. Aren't you?

I love you, and that is 100% fact. I love you, and I need you. You love me, and you need me, too. We need each other in our lives. We are blood. Your blood runs through me, and my blood runs through you. We are forever connected.

I am tired. Aren't you?

God forgave me. God forgave you. I forgive you. Will you forgive me?

We can let bygones be bygones. Differences and hurts can become like water under the bridge.

41

All the hurtful words we uttered at each other were meant to tear us apart - leave us in shreds - kill our souls - grind us like powder and bring us to our knees in pain. So, let's stay on our knees in prayer against the enemy that comes only to steal, kill and destroy. Greater is He that is in us than he that is in the world. Let us replace all the words we have used to hurt each other with God like words that are only meant to build us up - make us strong and worthy. Words confirming that even though we are not perfect, either of us, we are worthy of each other's love.

I admit I am tired. Will you admit that you are tired, too?

Can we give this relationship the chance it deserves?

Reflections

_____

_____

JUST SAYIN

There are more two-way streets around than there are one - way streets.

Even though you are moving fast and forward on that one- way street,

You never know when you will have to exit and come back to that two-way street.

Just Sayin

Reflections

_____

_____

RELAX

When life overwhelms you with so much stuff

that it says you have to do

Right Now - Today

Just remember, all you really have to do

Right now – Today

Is to love God and to love your neighbor as you love yourself

God has everything else in His hands

Relax - You can rest in Him

Reflections

_____

_____

NOT WITHOUT MERCY

Not one of us lives a single day without God's mercy

Let us forgive as we have been forgiven

Be merciful as we have been shown mercy

Not man's mercy that changes as easily as the direction of the wind

but the mercy of God that never changes

And because of this mercy, He never reminds us of our sins

that he has thrown into the sea of forgetfulness

Reflections

_____

_____

THE THING

Gods' word will accomplish what He pleases and make the thing
He sends it to prosper.

"Lord, let me be the thing to which Your word is sent, that I may
prosper in my relationship with You and in every area of my life.

Let me prosper in everything that concerns me because I know,
that which concerns me, also concerns you.

Reflections

_____

_____

ADEQUATE

You cannot make yourself adequate

Only through Me can you become adequate

I, and I alone, make you adequate

Reflections

_____

_____

ONE STOP SHOP

There is no doubt that people, young or old, can be cruel

When the cruelties of this world try to overtake you, and you just want to hide,

remember that you have a hiding place in the word of God

It is the one-stop shop for all you will ever need

Reflections

_____

_____

EITHER

People will or they won't

People can or they can't

People do or they don't

Either way, let it be okay

Reflections

_____

_____

TRAGEDY STRIKES

It has been one year today since my son was in that awful car accident, an accident that left him changed for life (unless the Lord intervenes on his behalf) Some changes are visible to all, but the changes that have taken place that are most important are only visible to those that know him best. There are some changes only a mother can see - not a father - sister, or brother - only a mother.

Life can totally change for all of us in a matter of seconds. It always happens to other people, not to us. Isn't that the way most of us go through life, thinking that no one or anything can touch us and that nothing can alter our own little perfect world we have created for our families and ourselves? How foolish we are, how very foolish.

It was a Monday afternoon in September 1989. We had just returned a few days prior from the funeral of my grandmother. My son had come home from Kentucky on emergency leave to be with his great-grandmother before she passed. He had started to return that day but, for some unknown reason, decided to leave the next day instead. How I wished he had done as his mind first led him - how often I have wished.

I was at work that day when he stopped by and asked for a few dollars so he and his friends could go to Charlotte and check out some girls. I remember telling him to stay home and if he would not stay home to at least not take his car to go out of town. He said he would not take his car, he would ride with friends – the last ride he would take for many months to come.

Shortly after I arrived from work, he and three of his friends came. They packed the car, and off they went on a ride that would alter every one of their lives.

A feeling of uneasiness –of anxiousness seemed to engulf me that afternoon, and I didn't know why. It was about 9pm or a little later when the brother of one of his friends knocked on my door and asked if I knew where my son was. I told him that he was not here. He had left earlier with his friends. He turned around and left the door, but it was as if he already knew something but hoped that what he knew was not true.

I watched him as he got into his mother's car. A feeling of strangeness about his being there - the look on his face - the tone of his voice when he asked where my son was. Something was not right. I saw his mother get out of the car. The look on her face assured me that what I was feeling and what I was thinking was true. I wanted to close the door in her face -   to forget that she was there –to not let her inside - to not hear what I knew she was going to say. At the same time, I knew I had to hear it no matter how bad - I had to know. The way she said my name was as if she were bracing me for something, and that was enough for panic to set in. 'Where is your son?" I told her that he was with his friends, her son included. There goes that sound again, the sound of her calling my name. She had received a phone call from the Hamlet, NC Police Dept, and there had been an accident.

I just looked at her, wishing she would go away. I could not speak - not yet. I had to hear more. I knew the worst had not yet been spoken. She informed me of what she knew. Her son and another young man were doing pretty well. They had taken one of the other young men to Duke Hospital immediately. There was no time to waste with him. The problem was that they did not know which one it was. There were no IDs to identify who was who, and they could not speak for themselves. They didn't know anything. The other young man was at Moore County Hospital in Pinehurst.

Which way to go - where to go - which one was my son? These were the questions that crossed and filled my mind. I didn't know. I only knew that I had to get out of this house and go in some direction. I had to know where my son was - how bad was he - had he died since I became aware of the accident?

I dressed. I really did not know how to get to either place, Pinehurst or Durham, but I chose to go to Pinehurst. Whether I chose it because it was closer or because I was hoping against hope that it would be my son that even in critical condition, they did not feel the urgency to have to rush him by helicopter to Duke. I don't know.

Anyway, I reached a friend who knew the Pinehurst area, met her and began my journey. I was silent during the ride. She talked and tried to encourage me along the way. Her words were like water going through a sifter. I heard them - they meant nothing, absolutely nothing to me. My son, my son, was all that meant anything to me at that moment.

We reached the ER and told them why we were there. A nurse ran into the back, informing the Dr. that the possible mother of the patient had arrived and was out front. I could feel the urgency in her voice. It was as if they had been waiting for someone, for me, before some enormous decision could be made. I did not want to be the one they were waiting for.

Once there, I did not want to know who was back there. I did not want to know what his condition was. I wanted to be back home safe - content, but I couldn't. I was here; I had to go on.

Immediately, with the swiftness of a rushing wind, we were taken back to a waiting room. As we were entering, I glimpsed through a window in a door. Someone was on a bed thrashing around - moaning - unable to find peace or comfort for their body. I could not see the face, but the voice producing only sounds, sounds of pain, was undeniably the voice of my son. Two feelings engulfed me at once, if that is at all possible. Relief that he was not rushed to Duke and fear that something was terribly wrong. The look on the

Dr.'s face confirmed my feeling of fear. I looked at him without really seeing him as he told me that my son's leg had to be amputated. He would save as much as he possibly could, but too much time had passed, and his life was on the line.

No choice; a consent form was put in front of me. I could hardly see it, much less read it, with all the tears falling from my eyes. No sounds came from my mouth, but inside, I could hear shouting so much shouting. The words finally came. I don't remember exactly what they were, but I knew everything inside of me was denying this whole situation.

It was a dream, yes, that is what it was, a terrible dream, and soon I would awaken, and everything would be back to normal. A nurse's voice urging the Dr to return to my son woke me from my fantasy. It was not a dream. It was real. No one was going to wake me up; no one would rescue me from this harsh - horrid reality.

He is only 20 years old. This can't be true. How – why - what happened - how can this be - why my son? All the obvious questions came to fill my mind at once. There would be time for questions later. Now my consent was needed. NOW! I looked again at the paper as if it were some foreign object; what was I supposed to do with it?

Did I have the right to sign something that would alter his life so extensively, so radically? Would he rather die than live without one of his limbs? I didn't know; I could not ask him. There was no one that could answer me. I was alone - totally alone. It was as if even God had forsaken me and would not give me an answer. My name - my signature was needed. I finally managed to write on the paper, "The paper". The paper that meant life or death for my son. Done - it was done - no turning back.

It was hours before we received any word on his condition. My husband and my two other sons had arrived since the consent form had been signed. We were now waiting upstairs in a waiting room on the floor to which he would be brought. Would he be brought here - would he make it? There go those questions again. At that moment, I hated questions with passion because I had no answers.

He finally did arrive critically, but alive. "Thank You, God" was all I could say. He was alive, but I could sense the presence of death. Even though I could not feel His presence, My God was always there. "Hope, why did you leave, -Faith, where did you go?" All the things I had believed in and was always so quick to encourage others had failed me. I could not believe - I could not.

He was connected to all kinds of equipment. He was not breathing on his own. Would he ever breathe on his own again?

Go away, questions, go away. The Dr informed us that he was indeed still in critical condition and that how he responded in the next few days would be crucial in whether he would survive. He had done all he could with what he had. He had managed for now to keep it a below the knee amputation, but it could change at any moment to an above the knee amputation.

The leg was so badly mangled and filled with all kinds of debris. There was dirt – trash - pine straw, and glass. Infection was inevitable. The only question was if they could keep it at a minimum - if they could keep it under control - if they could keep him alive. If, if, if a word I began to hate.

I finally went home - I did not want to go home - I did not want to leave my son, my firstborn. I arrived home. I don't know how or when I got there, but I was there. A good friend had come prepared to stay all night with the rest of my children. Somehow, I had forgotten about the other children. Now, I remembered. Forgive me, God.

When I saw my friend sitting on the couch, just waiting to be told what she could do and how she could help, I began to cry because she could not comfort me. There was nothing she could do or say to make me feel better as much as I knew she wanted to.

Somehow, I made it through the night and returned to the hospital first thing in the morning. Things were the same, only he should have been coming around by now. He must have had a head injury, was the thought of his Dr., and X-rays proved the thought to be true. He had a severe concussion.

The days were filled with emptiness for me. Family and friends came and went. Calls – cards - so many caring people - caring gestures - words of hope. Yet, I was alone, and no one could penetrate the private world I had created for us. No one understood - no one felt the pain - no one could help. At least, that was my feeling at the time.

Unintentionally, so very unintentionally, I began to close out my husband, the love and strength of my life and my children, my true support system, the pieces of my heart. If they felt any kind of way, any resentment or jealousy, they never let it be known. They loved - they cared - they cried - they were afraid, too. Again, my focus was on my son. He was all that mattered –the rest of the world could take care of itself.

Finally, he began to come around writing horrible things on paper that a mother's eyes should never see. Things like "I feel dead." "Am I dead?" "I am dead like Nana." (My grandmother) I assured him that he was not dead, although to me, the presence of death was still very real.

Infection had truly set in, and they were consulting with medical facilities all over the country, as well as the CDC desperately trying to obtain the right cocktail of meds to combat the infection. Things were still not stable. He had to be taken to the OR every other day to have his stump cleaned of more debris. As a result of the infection, a very odorous aroma constantly filled the room no matter how well and often it was sanitized. He became very depressed by the stench of the room. Have you ever smelled the stench of death?

We finally had to tell him of the death of his friend, the driver of the car that fateful night. He cried and seemed to take that news harder than the news of his amputation.

Thinking back to that time now, he had made it; he was alive, and there was still hope for him. PRAISE GOD!

As he progressed, he was transferred to Ft. Bragg before being airlifted to Walter Reed in Washington, DC, where he finally, after months of skin grafts, received his first prosthesis.

The healing process of his leg had begun, and he made it through, but the healing of his mind - his heart - his soul had not yet begun. It would take a lifetime for that process to begin, and it may never fully end.

There have been some rough times for all of us, especially him. There have been periods of denial on his part – ours as well. He has changed; he is not the same. The physical is obvious to all who know him. The emotional changes, again, only to those who know him best.

What a difference a day - an hour - a moment - a second can make in our lives. My sons' life changed - my life changed - my husbands' life changed - my children's lives changed. There is something different about all our lives, not visible to the average onlooker but quite noticeable to us. For in a true family, what affects one, somehow affects all - it should.

We have come through so many stages during our tragedy, but we have remained strong and intact. I have learned –we have learned that none of us is immune to tragedy - to hurt - to pain - to change and that it does not always happen to someone else's family. It sometimes happens to yours.

Reflections

_____

_____

SHARON BARBEE SIMMONS

THE BEST

You may not understand it

You may not agree with it

But this IS the best I can do right now

Reflections

_____

_____

I FORGET

- Where I put things
- What you told me last month, last week, yesterday, maybe even earlier today
- What I told you in those same periods of time
- Appointments
- Things I was supposed to do
- Birthdays

SOMETIMES I JUST FORGET

- Ages - yours - grandchildren – friends - even mine
- Grades - who is in what grade whose graduation did I miss?
- Accomplishments - I used to remember what all of you did

THINGS I NEVER SHOULD FORGET, BUT I DO

MY FORGETFULNESS IS:

- Not intentional
- Not meant to hurt
- Not meant to frustrate
- Not meant to aggravate
- Not meant to make uneasy
- Not meant to try your patience

SHARON BARBEE SIMMONS

I JUST FORGET

- To call your name on the first second or maybe even the fifth try
- To accurately relay messages or relay them at all
- To check messages-e-mails-much less respond to them
- About the package, the delivery man was going to bring. Sorry I forgot

MY FORGETFULNESS, I PRAY:

- Will never get worse
- Will not let me forget what my name is or who I am

- Will never let me forget who you are
- Will never let me forget that I am your mother (father, son, daughter or whatever relation)
- Will never let me forget that you are my children and the very pieces of my heart
- Will never let me forget that I love God - even more that God loves me
- Will never let me forget that love is all I have ever had for all of you

FORGIVE MY FORGETFULNESS

- If I ever say words that hurt - I won't mean them
- If I can't find the door even though you have shown me many times

THIS ONE'S JUST 4 U

- If I can't tie my shoes or even know what shoes looks like regardless of how many times you have put them on my feet
- If I don't know, after all the meals I have cooked, what a stove looks like or what function it serves.
- If my house is a mess because I don't know where things belong or can't remember that I was going to clean and straighten things up
- If I don't remember anything or anyone that you think I should. Please don't get angry with me because I really don't remember it or them

IN ALL MY FORGETFULNESS, PLEASE KNOW...

- That I love you
- That I am here somewhere, amid all this forgetfulness
- That I am praying that you won't get tired of trying to find me
- That you can continue to look for me as long as you believe that I may come back to you

BUT PLEASE KNOW THIS...

- That when you decide that it is time to stop trying to find someone who is obviously no longer there - (me)

IT IS OKAY!!

- I give you permission with no guilt attached that you can stop looking now.

- Just never forget or stop loving the person I used to be, the person you used to know

  MOM

Reflections

_____

_____

HEAD OF THE HOUSE

The head of the house sometimes eats last

The head of the house sometimes doesn't eat at all

The head of the house always puts family first

Reflections

_____

_____

I KNOW YOU

People may not know you

You may not even know you

But I know you and love you

And all that comes with you

Reflections

_____

_____

64

NEED

He never needs me, but

He always wants me

Sometimes in my foolishness

I don't want Him

But I always need Him

Reflections

_____

_____

POWER OF THE RIB

When I called the heavens and the earth, I spoke them into being. I formed man and breathed the breath of life into him. I breathed into man's nostrils because yours were too delicate.

I allowed a deep sleep to come over man so that he would not interfere with My creativity. From one bone, I fashioned you. I chose the bone that protects man's life. I chose the strong yet delicate rib which protects him. His lungs support him as you are meant to do.

Your characteristics are as the ribs strong yet, delicate and fragile. You provide protection for his most delicate organs. His heart is the center of his whole being. His lungs hold the breath of life. The rib cage will allow itself to be broken before it will allow damage to the heart and lungs.

I wanted man to know all I fashioned in you - My holiness - My strength - My purity – My love – My support, and My protection. You are special because you are an extension of me.

Man represents My image. Woman - My emotions. Together you represent the totality of Me. So, man, treat the woman well. Love her - respect her, for she is fragile. In hurting her, you hurt me. What you do to her, you do to me (good or bad). In crushing her, you damage your own heart and lungs.

Woman, support man as the rib cage. In humility, show him the power of emotion that I have given to you. In gentle quietness, show your strength. In love, show him that you are the rib that protects his inner strength, his inner self and that he without a doubt, needs you.

Reflections

_____

_____

SUCH A GOOD KID

Guess what? Every family has one - Such a good kid. Does that surprise you? It shouldn't.

So many times, the "Such a good kid" is easily overlooked just for that very reason – they are such a good kid.

It is never because you don't love them, never because of that. Maybe we don't see them in the way we see the other children because they are somehow not like the other children at all.

They seem to require so much less hands-on than the rest of the children. "Seem to" is the key phrase, so don't breeze by that as you read.

You never constantly have to remind them of what they should be doing. Very seldom do you find a reason to chastise them because when everything else is in fighting and chaos mode, they are usually the ones trying to smooth things over or quietly sitting in a chair staring at all this stuff unfolding.

The phone does not ring - notes don't come home about any improper behavior for this child. You never have to constantly intervene for them because they always seem to be in complete control. "Seem to be" They don't need you by their side every moment, hardly ever, as a matter of fact.

To you, they appear happy – self-sufficient - in need of nothing and never getting too involved in family stuff.

Let me share something with you that I found out the hard way and way too late. They (these good kids) are not always what they appear to be or how we have chosen to perceive them. Maybe it just made it easier for us - one less thing or child to worry about.

They need - they long for that pat on the back - that extra touch - hug just for them. Not a big group hug where everyone is included. They need a just you and them hug- no one else included. They long for extra time with you. They want to hear those "I Love Yous." that we just figured they knew. Figuring out is not enough. SHOW – TELL - TOUCH - HUG – KISS - TALK – PLAY

They are silently screaming to you – to us parents, "See me,"- "Make me first today." – "I am here, too." - "I need you."

If we don't address this kid now and continue to wait and act as if nothing is wrong, you will wake up one day and realize that the perfect relationship you thought you had was not - it was just a show, and it is starting to disintegrate before your very eyes, and you are wondering why.

It is that "good kid" saying without speaking a word, "You failed me." – "You messed up." - "Something was lacking." Maybe we could have done something so simple as posting a Keep Out - this is a private party for just me and my mom or me and my dad sign on the door.

They have lost their place – their position in the family that should have rightfully been theirs, and you never even noticed. My Lord, what does that say about us? Were we so busy with life and other children that we failed to remember that they, too, were children and not adults? They were our babies that never used their voices to make themselves known or voice their true opinions about the things that mattered to them.

We have somehow overlooked their value - their genius - their insight - their empathy, and all that they have added to this family. I, for one, am so very sorry and ashamed.

They are grown now, and the harm has been done, but it is not too late to fix some of it. We never get to have do-overs, but we do get second attempts to try and lessen the damage of some of our mistakes. Take them in your arms even if they struggle a bit (they really want this). Tell them you love them - you have always loved them - you will always love them, and for any hurt – pain - confusion – feelings of low self-esteem or any failure to obtain their fullest potential you have caused them, you are beyond sorry and you beg their forgiveness, praying all the time for total and complete restoration that only God can give.

Do it now - don't wait. Save both that "Such a Good Kid" and yourself years of future heartache and irreconcilable differences. You don't want this kid to never be in your life because of the foolish mistakes you have made. It can happen - it does happen. Don't let it happen to you.

"It's me and you Kid."

Reflections

_____

_____

NO TIME LIKE NOW

We have all heard and no doubt spoken the repeated adage "Tomorrow is not promised to us." Well, nor is the next second - moment - hour or day. So, take a moment right now to text – call- email or visit someone and tell them you love them - that they are important to you, and that you need them in your life. Let them know that you are glad they are a part of your life. I take this moment to say all these things to you because I do love you and I never want it to be said that I waited too late.

Reflections

_____

_____

IT TAKES A VILLAGE

It does not matter what corner of the earth you find yourself in, "No man is an island." as said by John Donne (1572-1631).

I piggyback on his quote when it comes to children whether they be in our homes – neighborhoods - cities, or any other place in this world. No one person, whether it be a parent - a teacher - a coach or anyone else, pours into all the entities that make up a child. It takes a village to raise a child. We all have a role to play and an obligation to play that role. You – me - all of us.

No one person can meet every need of every child –for it takes a myriad of experiences – education – talents - been there-done that mentality, and most of all a willingness to be my brother's keeper no matter their age.

You must deny yourself and give to that child - that little person. Maybe you are the one that makes sure they get fed every day. Someone else is making sure they have those eyeglasses they need so that they will be able to see the board at school. You may be the hugger and that is all that you can give but you are the best hugger in the world to them.

Are you the one that shows up for all the after-school sports activities? That one that has been so constant that they have even stopped looking for their real mom or dad's face. They just squint their eyes until they see your face, and they know that all is well because you are there. You could be the one that makes sure they are on time for school because Mom must leave early for work to provide what little she can for the family. You also make sure they get home from school safe and sound because Dad has no car and sometimes works overtime. Oh, and don't forget about the mom that is always there making sure every child gets acknowledged and sees a smiling face. The one that always has a snack of some kind for all of them even though she only has one child participating.

Whatever part you are playing in this "It Takes a Village to Raise a Child," keep playing it - invite a few more Villagers to answer the call. Call a few more children that need to be served by the village. You see them - they are easily spotted. The one that is always trying to be included but never seems to get close enough. The one that never looks happy - is always being avoided by the other kids because their clothes or shoes are not quite up to par and always seems hungry. You know them - probably passed by them a hundred times. They may even live in your neighborhood –your complex or go to your church.

Encourage some of the moms – dads - grandparents that can't give as much as others and take the time to find out what they can give. It may be that on weekends they could share some of their heritage - their traditions - cooking skills - even a second language. Who wouldn't love to learn another language?

We all have something we can do well. God made sure of that.

Now we have this BIG village where you can finally share your God - given talent with someone to whom it may mean the world one day - maybe even today. It may even change their life and the life of another villager, as each one pays forward that which was freely given to them.

You are the village.

Reflections

_____

_____

HELPING

You are doing all this added stuff in this situation because you think you are helping God out?

Wow! I would love to see the look on His face right about now

He is LOL for real!

Reflections

_____

_____

USED TO BE

Well, yeah, you - me and everyone else used to be something

Drunks-Whores-Midnight Ramblers-Liars-Murderers-Abusers of men-women and children

Back Biters- Disobedient-Untrustworthy-Two faced-Sexually Immoral

I would most likely take up this entire page if I were to name all the things we used to be-

But you know what?

Used to be - Ain't no more

THAT IS THE DIFFERENCE

Don't let anyone put you back into that box

JESUS HAS TAKEN YOU OUT OFF!!

Reflections

_____

_____

FAMILY MATTERS

Submit to one another out of reverence for Christ. Submission is in direct opposition to our flesh's desire to rule and have its way.

We defend our rights - champion our causes - speak passionately about our opinions, and assert our own agendas whenever possible. God's way is to crucify our flesh and submit to the needs and wishes of others whenever possible. Jesus is our model or should be, for that kind of submission to God's will. For when they hurled insults at Him, He did not retaliate. When He suffered, He made no threats. Instead, He entrusted Himself to Him, who judges justly.

Most family problems could be lessened - not necessarily done away with completely if we follow the instructions: Do nothing out of vain conceit or self-ambition. Rather in humility, value others above yourself - not looking to your own interest but each of you to the interest of others.

When we adopt the spirit of humility and treat others as Jesus would treat them - no matter who they are or what they have done to hurt us, we can resolve many of our family and relationship problems.

Do we agree that we all have some faults and share some blame in all that has taken place? Do we all agree that we have not made every Godly effort, not manly effort where tempers fly and hurt words get said to resolve them? Do we all agree that we want to resolve these differences, which may mean taking responsibility for what you may or may not feel belongs to you but may be the perception of another person? Remember, a person's perception is their truth, and so is yours.

Will we today declare and decree that upon this rock (Jesus) our family is built, and the very gates of hell shall not prevail against it - against us? Each one for the other.

Reflections

_____

_____

JESUS AIN'T SCARED OF YOUR SIN

We, as a people in general, are afraid of sin, more likely the person who commits the sin. I just want to say to the "BIG SINNER" of course, there is no "BIG SINNER". Sin is sin, no matter how you look at it.

Jesus looks you and your sin straight in the eye – face to face. He ain't scared, and He ain't running from you. You know why? Cause your sin ain't nothing to him – nothing. He can handle it. He died for your sin. Your sin does not make him tremble, and there is nothing you have done that was not and is not covered by His shed Blood.

This does not mean that you can do what you want - when you want - to whom you want - that you can have free reign with sin, and you have no need to worry. "Nah" that ain't how this works. You can't go around doing what you are doing and think that God has you covered and that you are straight.

Godly sorrow worketh repentance, and if you are truly sorry and never intend to do any of the horrible things you may have done to people - to yourself and to God again, then God has His Son standing right there in front of you, and He is not flinching.

If you accept Him as your Lord and Savior - admit that you are a sinner and that you no longer want to live the life you have been living-confess with your mouth the Lord Jesus and believe in your heart that God raised Him from the dead you are now saved with all the rights and responsibilities of being a child of the Most High God.

He won't leave you like people you thought wouldn't but did. He will never leave you or forsake you. His loyalty is 100% genuine - no fakeness about it.

So, do not conform to this world - be transformed by the renewing of your mind.

Let Him give you a new mind and a new heart.

Reflections

_____

_____

BEYOND

God works in and on the beyond.

People who seem to us to be beyond help – hope - salvation - deliverance - healing - forgiveness, and so on. This is where God performs His best work.

Isn't it where He found you?

If you think you are "beyond", then you are in the right place for God to show Himself mighty to you.

Reflections

_____

_____

FROM NIGGA TO BLACK

Why? Why are you so afraid of us? What have we ever done to you?

It was you that dragged our ancestors from their "Motherland" - the only home and land that they had ever known. Were they asked – did they have a choice? "NO" they were just roped together men - women - children and cargoed over in the filthiest and most inhumane conditions the mind could imagine to the place you called "The White Man's World."- a place of which they had no knowledge of what was there or what horrible conditions and changes of life awaited them. I wonder what thoughts crossed their minds – what amount of fear encompassed them not only for them individually but for them as a united people accustomed to always being together - always being united?

And for what reason did you do this - why did you feel the need to disrupt the heritage of an entire people? Of course, the answer is easy enough - because that was the way you, white man, wanted it to be, and so it was. How much money was a soul - a life - the eradication of families worth to you? You may not have known then, but I assure you that you will know in the future that no amount of money could buy us - could break us. Because we were- are and always will be strong people.

What was it about us – the strength of our bodies, the blackness of our skin that impressed you, even though you would never admit it?

Did you look at your own delicate skin color and weak body structure and realize that there was no comparison between the two? You just could not imagine yourself doing what you wanted to be done, what you wanted our bodies to do in your stead. You knew that under the duress - the fear of your whip - the many unknowns from being in a strange place and having no knowledge of how to return to their home, they would do whatever you wanted - however you wanted - whenever you wanted while you sat back and reaped the benefits of forced labor that cost us our lives and much more than that - our dignity.

You did for a while - 400 plus years to be exact, but we were - are and always will be a strong people. We endured with closed mouths for a very long time, hours and hours in the scorching and blazing sun. No breaks - no lunch - just work. Working constantly – too fearful to rest. Still not enough for the "Massa."

Surely all of that should have earned us something on the scale of humanness. My mistake. What about all the beatings - maimings - lynches – shootings - castrations of our black men? Surely seeing how we withstood these injustices should have earned us something someplace on the scale of humanness. Again, my mistake. This was still not enough for "Massa".

"Studs" - that is all our black men were in the eyes of the white man. They were strong - virile - huge - versatile - black-skinned studs that could sire many future studs who would one day be as strong, if not stronger than their fathers, and this tradition would be repeated forever. At least that is what you thought, but we were – are and always will be strong people.

Many babies born on the plantation? Yes. Born to be free? Certainly not these. These are going to be owned by one "Massa" or another for the rest of their lives. Told what to do - how to do - where to do - when to do, at least that is what you thought, but we were - are and always will be strong people.

How much more does it take for you to see some humanness in us? All of these things should have earned us something. Again, my mistake.

Our women, who were beautiful - strong - smooth - black skinned - wide - hipped, and thick-haired were secretly being visited in the night - even in the day - just depended on when "Massa" got the urge. They were being forced to let him possess the most precious part of them - the part of them that was always meant to be shared with that one black man that she loved and for whom she had saved herself. She was beaten and whipped if she dared to resist - left feeling degraded - humiliated and unworthy to give herself to her man, but despite all she endured, he loved her still and knew that neither of them had the power to prevent this - not at that time. For what man now or then could have endured the mere thought of another man violating his woman? Still, this price paid was not enough. What could possibly be enough for you, white man? God knows I have no idea.

Well, how about our fair-skinned - good-haired - green or blue-eyed sisters and brothers that were born out of those secret visits in the night and day? Mothers black – fathers white baby still a "Nigga." Still hidden from the "Massas'" wife.

Our women were in your houses giving suck to your babies. Your babies sucked the milk of our babies' mothers' breasts. Some of our babies were being suckled by mothers who were not their own. Not enough milk for both white and nigga child, too. Who was left out - who died? You answer the question?

Still not enough? Of course, not. What about watching our sons - daughters - husbands - wives - mothers - fathers taken from us without any thought or concern for our feelings – our hurt - the emptiness that it was causing inside of us. Remind you of anything still going on in this world we live in today where our black men are being incarcerated and killed most of the time for just being black. They are different circumstances, or maybe not so different, but the outcome is the same. We are still left broken - lost - hurt and angry.

Never going to change, or so you thought - you think. We were- are and have always been strong people.

Aha! Finally, slavery was over but don't forget that they "forgot" to tell our brothers and sisters in Texas the truth for another two years. How do you forget that – how do you explain that to an already suffering people? You can't – you simply can't. You still did not – do not want us to be free even with all the contributions to this country that you call your own we have made.

We never bothered you, but your fear of us has continued to show - to grow. You wanted us to stay down. No education for us - no justice for us - nothing at all for us.

Well, "No more." We are determined. Destined to rise to every occasion - every challenge that is put before us, for we were - are and always will be a strong people.

We are Pastors - Bishops – Scientists - Teachers - Writers - Senators - CEOs - Judges - Authors - Psychologists - Dentists - Doctors - Architects - Artists - White Collar Workers - Blue Collar Workers, too. The list goes on and on.

Everywhere you are, we are. Look beside you – behind you - to the left of you - to the right of you, and especially in front of you. We are in your neighborhoods - workplaces - county clubs - golf courses - boardrooms - your isolated islands, or so you thought. You name it, we are there, or we can be IF we choose to be. You see, we now have the right to choose - we have choices. Some of you even work for us - we yo boss.

Did you ever even think that when you took our people from their homes – tribes - cities – nations - that you were removing Kings - Queens – Princes and Princesses that were established long before any of you? - that you were trying to destroy destinies that had long before you been established? Destiny can never be destroyed. You didn't and don't have that power.

It took a while to get where we are, and there is still a long way to go but be assured beyond measure of this:

No more will we endure your inhumane treatment of us. No longer will our babies die so that yours will live. No longer will we believe that you are better than us. No longer will we believe that we have no minds - no imaginations - no dreams that we cannot make into reality.

Fear if you must, but it is time for you to face the fact and to know without any question in your heart that we have come from Nigga to Black, and we won't ever go back.

For we were - are and always have been a strong people. So, see us now as we were always meant to be seen - A STRONG BLACK PEOPLE of KINGS and QUEENS.

Reflections

_____

_____

IN MY FATHER'S HOUSE

I am always welcome in my father's house - be it a closet – a spot on the floor - a place on my bed - in the shower – in the car - even in the kitchen - anywhere.

Anywhere He is becomes His house, and I am always welcome. I can come and sit in His presence, ask Him to surround me with His love, even put me in a bubble sometimes and quiet all the outside noises - voices - situations and problems that are trying to invade our privacy - our time together.

Being a good Father, He does just that. He keeps guard over me – a special guard at these times. No one gets in when I am in my father's house.

If you have a good God given earthly father, you know that what Daddy says goes. You may buck for a few minutes, but you know when to calm down and STOP IT.

When my Father speaks, IN THE NAME OF JESUS, all interfering thoughts must cease. Calmness is commanded and immediately prevails.

In my Father's house - I am safe - I am free - I am me - His child guaranteed the peace that surpasses all understanding - all human understanding.

There is no place I would rather be. A place where no one or anything else matters - only being in His presence.

We can't stay there forever - not yet, and live in this world, too. We must come out sometime to face the realities of this world and life. But thank God, as often as I want, I can come into my Father's house, and so can you because you, too, are invited.

Reflections

I WONDER

There are times when I spend hours - days wondering what you think about me

Today is not one of them

Reflections

_____

_____

DISAPPOINTED

Though I may be thoroughly disappointed in myself or yes, even in you, God is never disappointed in us. "Why not?" you would probably want to know.

Disappointment on God's side would mean that He did not know our beginning - our end and everything in between. But He did - and does know. To be disappointed in someone you must have never expected a certain action or behavior out of them. That is not God. He expects and knows every action - reaction - behavior - attitude and language that we will ever display; therefore, no disappointment can present itself to Him.

He may be saddened for us when we go the wrong direction taking longer to get to where He has called us to be, but He is not disappointed.

All sins were forgiven, right? We believe that, but then days come when we start to wonder if we are enough because of mistakes - wrong choices that we sometimes make even after being forgiven. Our downfalls do not prevent Jesus from loving us or saying that He gave His life for us and that we were and are worth it. We must believe that we are enough, for He makes us enough.

Release disappointment of yourself and anyone else you are holding to an unattainable standard, and believe that God is not disappointed in you and that He loves you.

Reflections

_____

_____

MOTIVES

God knows what you do

And why you do it

Check your motives

Reflections

I CALL YOU HOME

Today, I call you home. It does not matter what it looks like to the outside world. Who it looks like had the power to take you out - the power to make you leave this earth.

I CALL YOU HOME

When I call you home, there is no one or anything that can keep you in this place.

You belong to Me First

You belong to Me always.

TODAY, I CALL YOU HOME

You are at rest now. No more looking over your shoulder - sleeping with one eye opened - imagining the worst that could ever happen to you. No more imagining - it has happened - it is over.

I CALL YOU HOME

No more concerns about tomorrow for all of your tomorrows from this day and forever are with Me. You are forever resting with Me - in Me.

I CALL YOU HOME

There is no better place for you to be than with Me. I saw your tears - your fears - your concerns about things and people that you could never seem to change nor manage to make the necessary detachment you wanted so much to make. I heard your prayers. Even when no one else knew you were praying, I knew.

I CALL YOU HOME

Because I love you, and I knew that even though you may have looked fine to everyone else - even to those who loved you best and will miss you the most. I knew you were tired – worn - weary and afraid on the inside. I felt your pain and fear so strongly that I knew it was time and the best place - the only place for you was with Me. So, today,

I CALL YOU HOME

TO REST - TO BE FREE - TO FOREVER BE WITH ME

Reflections

_____

_____

WITHOUT YOU

I am finding myself in a place that I have never been before

A place somewhere that I could never imagine being. Someplace that I never knew existed, much less that could make me feel this way

What is this place? Where is this place?

I feel empty - numb - frozen - lost

My head is in a fog –a dream state. My mind can't fathom this

Part of me knows that it is real

Part of me refuses to accept this place in which I find myself a prisoner

You are gone

No, that cannot be - it cannot be

What will I do? Who am I without you?

I don't know - I cannot remember a time that you have not been a part of my life

Any time before you, ceased to exist when you entered my world

Years - decades we have been two, even with others around that we loved, it was always us two - just the two of us

I don't know how to say goodbye to you

I don't know right now how I will ever make it without you

Without calling your name out for one thing or another

Without knowing that you are just in the next room

Without snuggling under you in bed when the covers are just not enough

Without you loving - touching - caressing and kissing me and without me being able to do the same to you

How will I make it without making sure you are okay when you are not feeling well?

Without you making sure that I am okay when I am not feeling well?

Without our both thinking and saying the same thing at the same time and bursting out laughing when no one else knows why Wow! That was so much fun - just another you and I secret that I will miss - How can I make it without you?

How can I make it without you and all the strength you posessed for the both of us? I always leaned on you when I had no strength of my own

How can I make it without the understanding that no one else had of me but you? You always understood and accepted me for me Thank you

I don't know how I will be able to begin without you

I don't know when I will be able to begin without you

I only know that the you I love would want me to go on with my life

The you I love would never want me to stop living my life or put it on hold

The you I love would want me to survive and thrive in this world without you

So, because of the respect and honor I have for you, I will try

It won't be easy, and it might take longer than you or anyone else might expect, but I promise my love, I will live in this world without you and make my mark however small or great for the both of us - only know that I will never stop missing and loving you

Reflections

_____

_____

WHIRLWIND

As the dawn of a New Year approaches, do not let us forget those that are in the middle of a whirlwind crying out "Lord, won't you reach down and snatch me out of this whirlwind long enough to let me think - to let me breathe?

I can't think - I can't hear your voice - I can't see. It is just darkness and wind. Whirling on top of whirling. I am being thrown to and fro - up and down.

I know I need to go right but left is the only direction I can manage to go. My mind is all messed up wanting to do what it wants even when I don't. I seem to have a will but no power to escape.

When I desire to speak loving - kind - soothing – encouraging words, all I can hear are words that are harsh - cold - hurtful and unfeeling. Words that would break the heart - soul and spirit of any human being.

When I want to love - caress - hold - be held or show any affection, my fists go on the defense - coming into full view hitting walls - people and things. I hit - I hurt, but it is me that hurts the worst.

I can't control the things I don't want to do and cannot do the things I desire to do- the good things - the things that come only from You. SNATCH ME, LORD FROM THIS WHIRLWIND OF A PLACE. Hold me in Your hands where no one can lay hold on me

I don't want to be here anymore - I can't be here anymore. I am dying and all those that I love are dying with me just watching what is happening to me

Take all the evil fight out of me - remove me from people - circumstances - situations - conditions and choices that I, and I alone have made

You have had mercy on me so many times. This time, Lord, I believe is my last time and if You don't snatch me now and create in me a clean heart, I feel there will be no more chances for me

My time is running out. I see it every day. A living dog is better than a dead lion. What can I give You from the grave? What, Lord?

"SNATCH ME - SAVE ME AND I WILL FOREVER GIVE YOU PRAISE FOR ONLY WHAT YOU CAN DO. AMEN."

Reflections

CRAYONS

Sometimes you may get an imperfect box

Some may be broken in many pieces

Some may have peeling paper

Some may be sharp

Some may be dull

Some may need to be pressed down harder than others to get the
right color

Some may have one color written on them when in actuality, that
is not its true color

But even with all their differences and some seeming better than
others, they are all usable - we are all usable

Reflections

_____

_____

SSSH, LITTLE CHILD

Ssshh, little child for who would believe you anyway

Who would believe the one that everyone respects looks up to

Would ever do such a terrible thing to you

Ssshh, little child is what he says to you before he does what you know he will do

Ssshh, little child hold back those tears

Despite the pain and fear, he loves you

He says he does, and this is the way it is supposed to be

You belong to him and not another

Ssshh, little child you don't want your mama - sister - brother to be hurt

Besides where will you live if you tell - who will feed you - buy your clothes

Ssshh, little child as the nighttime visits turn into daytime visits as well

Each visit kills you a little more not only your body - but especially your soul

Ssshh, little child think of it no more -it won't stay with you forever

You can wash it away - it won't affect you for the rest of your life

Ssshh, little child your life can be whole. You will be able to love - to trust without any fear- without any reservation. He has done you no damage all of these years

No matter the cost - no matter the loss of people's love - the looks of unbelief

I will not Ssshh. I will tell and for the rest of my life I will be free

I will not be bound by what you have done to me

I will not protect you - someone should have protected me

I will not feel dirty - I will not feel shame

I will not Ssshh - I will tell

For the rest of my life, I will be free from all the horrible

things you have done to me

All of this is possible because I choose to forgive you

Forgiveness makes me free

Reflections

_____

_____

PROCRASTINATION

I am a procrastinator. Hmm, I wonder why? Why am I always putting off what I need to do not just until tomorrow not even to next week - next month or next year

It is not because I am lazy. I can surely tell you that.

I am not talking about making phone calls - grocery store runs washing clothes - cooking dinner - going to appointments and more. I have no problems with things like this, but when it comes to things that can change my life - things that can bring all of Gods' blessings into my life....

I PROCRASTINATE

Excellent and wonderful ideas and plans He gives me. Not only the plans but the gift of being able to carry out those plans. "Step out on the water," God says.

I PROCRASTINATE

I sometimes burst with anticipation of what He has told me that I am able to - do burst with anticipation for maybe a day or two then...

I PROCRASTINATE

With all of these wonderful things God has put in me, I wonder why...

I PROCRASTINATE

How much longer will He continue to give me the ability to do what He says I can do?

It is time to move and do what God says.

Motivated - motivated is what I am today. Ready to do all kinds of things. Things I have always wanted to accomplish.

I can do this - I know I can. I can't do it today, though. Surely by tomorrow I will be on my way, and I won't be turned aside by anything or anyone, even me.

Well, it is tomorrow. What can I say...

I PROCRASTINATE

Reflections

_____

_____

THINGS I NEVER HEAR FROM GOD

- I forgot
- I meant to
- I was going to but...
- It slipped my mind
- I remembered, then...
- Something happened
- I had to go somewhere
- Something came up
- I overslept
- I didn't feel well
- My alarm didn't go off
- It was too - hot too cold
- I just didn't get to it
- I changed my mind
- I had to be somewhere
- I had to make that money
- What happened was...
- I'll pick up the slack the next time
- You forgot to remind me

God never goes Ghost on you - Never

Try not to go Ghost on people that need and depend on you

Reflections

YOUR SPIRIT - YOUR BODY

I always wonder when someone dies why people say that they look just like themselves. I disagree - something is gone, something is missing, something is not there anymore.

The spirit, the real person, the real them is gone. It has gone back to the Father who gave it. We are never the same.

This body is just a physical holding place for who we really are, yet, we spend so much money and time on this holding place that we think is truly who we are. So little time - money - energy is spent on our real self - our spirit, the most valuable thing that we possess.

These bodies won't be going anywhere with us, no place eternal anyway, never. Yet, we fight so hard for them. Please, don't think of me as a hater. There is nothing wrong with looking good - exercising - taking care of your body, and eating healthy. Nothing at all wrong with that if you remember 1) a body is just what it is - made from dirt - will return to dirt 2) that looks will fade 3) strength will fail and 4) gravity always wins, just a part of God's plan.

Beauty-handsomeness may get you into some nice places- around some important people, but it won't save you - deliver you - find your favor (Gods'). It just won't.

Fight for your spirit - protect your spirit, feed your spirit. That is what will matter in the end. Who is the only one that is truly concerned about your spirit's eternal resting place? God is. He is the only one that can assure your eternal place when death comes, and your body, my brother - my sister, will have no more use for you. It will open no more doors for you - afford you no more great opportunities - make you special or make you adored by men and women. No. Time for that will be over. I pray you have taken good care of your spirit - It is really all you have.

Reflections

RESCUE ME

Rescue me from the thoughts that crowd my mind

Rescue me from the cares of this life

Rescue me when I feel like I am drowning and going down for the third and final time

Rescue me when all I seem to do is get it wrong

Rescue me when all I do is make it worse

Rescue me when I think I know what is best for me

Rescue me when I try to fix it my way

Rescue me whenever I think I know more about anything than You

Reflections

_____

_____

THE SONG WITHIN ME

I have heard that music can calm the savage beast, probably referring to the most fearless of all beasts - the most savage, the lion. I beg to differ and to say that sometimes that savage beast can be found in our minds.

You may at times hear the most beautiful music, vocals, instruments, the song that is number one all over the world, the one that everyone is on their feet jumping, singing, praising God and dancing to, but for you, it cannot pull your mind out of the place it is in.

Then comes this unknown - never heard of song out of your heart - your soul and not your mind. It is your God given song. It is meant only for you. No one else can sing it. No one else knows it. To the world, it can sound like 9 dying cats in a sack because it is only one of those songs your God can give you for such a time as this. A song that sets your mind free. God gives you the words, the tune, the rhythm and even the voice that you never had before.

It is that song that causes you to fall to your knees in worship after you have sung it over and over again for sometimes more than an hour-never missing a beat-a word and just dancing like no one was watching.

Now the song is over, and as my grandmother would say, I could not repeat one word of it -utter one phrase, or rock to the tune of it for all the tea in China. This song was given only to you by Him to free your mind at that time and for that moment. No one else's mind but yours.

For that one moment - one day to save you from the savage beast of your mind that was about to devour you.

Music will come again. It will come many times, but it won't be that music - never that music - never again for that time. Just know that He will save you many times from the savage beast playing in your mind. He loves you just that much, and He always watches and listens for you.

Just don't be afraid to sing the songs that are just for you from Him. Don't worry about remembering any of the ones from the last time...... He has more than enough songs just for you.

Reflections

_____

_____

I PROMISE

Happy Birthdate. You're here with all 10 fingers and toes. I'm so glad to finally meet you face to face. I have loved you from the first moment I knew about you, but no one could have prepared me for the love I feel at this moment. How can you love someone that you just met with this kind of love? I don't know; I only know that I do.

When I first saw you - held you in my arms and laid you on my chest, you looked so tiny - so small - so helpless, but I knew right then you were powerful enough to bring me to my knees now and always, and I thank God for you.

I don't know what the future holds. We will find that out together. I only promise you on this day that I will always love you and do my best to prove myself worthy of your love.

You're here. I'm here. We're here. Again, so glad to meet you.

Name of child:_____

Date of birth:_____

Parent signature:_____

Reflections

_____

_____

ALWAYS IN HIS LINE OF VISION

As I was praying today, a thought came to me, reminding me of how thankful I am to always be in Your line of vision.

I may be way over to the left or gone so far to the right that I can't be seen by a natural eye. To see me, people may have to move their head from the left - to the right - squint their eyes or maybe even bat or roll them a few times to get me into their focus. Now that is to get me into their natural line of vision. They have no clue that there is no chance of them finding me in a spiritual line of vision because of how far off the grid I have gone.

Not you, God. I am always in Your line of vision naturally and spiritually, even when I think I don't want You to see me. There are times when I feel like hiding from You - taking a little break - flying under the radar for a couple of moments - hours - days for some alone time, even from You.

Now, yes, I know that sounds crazy and impossible, but who says all my thoughts make sense, certainly not me.

Ah, but that is not happening, not with that sharper than an eagle eye of my Father. "Get back over here," He says.

"I see you, and I know you." and that He does. It takes too much wasted energy plotting - planning - ducking and hiding to try to do what you know you can't.

No matter where I am - how deep I think I have gone under - what I am doing while I am there, even the reason for my going, it is all there in His line of vision.

We have no surprises for God. Nothing we do - go through or changes of mind we may have, do not take Him by surprise. He knows us – always has known us - always will know us. We have been and forever will be in His line of vision.

Aren't you glad to know that He never loses sight of you and always knows just where you are - where to come and get you to save you - deliver and snatch you from the hand of the enemy? Have you ever been to some places that you were glad He knew where you were?

So, breathe a little sigh of relief knowing that He has your back and that you are always in His line of vision because He is in all places at all times. Be glad about that.

Reflections

_____

_____

FOOL ME

"Fool me. Act like you care." is something people say in jest, but maybe it is not just in jest.

Can a person be so desperate for attention - concern, and love that they will accept anything not to be left out?

Fake love - fake concern, and fake attention is what is being received. People are trying to get from others what can be gotten from You at no cost. No cost to their heart - their mind - their dignity, or their spirit because You freely give them all the attention - love and concern that they will ever need. No need for them to say to You, "Fool me."

Reflections

_____

_____

INTRODUCTIONS

I never had any trouble loving Jesus once I was properly introduced to Him and learned about His life - His Power - His Past and all that His future held for Him - for me.

My trouble came from my inability to believe that once He was introduced to me and learned of my life - my past and my almost non-existence of a future, He could never love me.

Funny thing is He needed no introduction to me. He already knew me from the beginning before I was ever conceived in my mothers' womb. My life from beginning - to middle - to end was no secret to Him. He knew it all, yet, He still wanted me to be introduced to Him.

Thank You for the introduction.

Reflections

_____

_____

FILLED WITH HOPE

As I begin to enter into a New Year with you, I am filled with the wonder of Your awesomeness and the anticipation of hope - dreams of destinies being fulfilled - prayers of yesterday, today, and tomorrow being answered - new beginnings - new things being done and calling those things that are not as though they were.

I am filled with the hope of hurts being healed - holes in my heart and soul being filled - broken promises and disappointments somehow being put out of my mind- healing for my soul - my life - my body - my marriage - my children - my family and my friends.

I am filled with the hope that You will strengthen me on the days that I grow weary and tired - Forgive me when I complain - Encourage me when my head hangs down - Remind me that You will never leave me or forsake me when I feel alone - Gently nudge me when I fail to pray for my enemies - Make me to know that I will reap what I sow, and although my reaping may take a while, it will come. I pray that when I feel like throwing up my hands, I will instead lift them in prayer.

I am filled with the hope of being more than a conqueror by taking back all the enemy has taken from me and that I have also given up without a fight sometimes. I have the hope of You always keeping Your hand upon me - Your blood always covering me - You always having my back - Your faithfulness and Your never changing love and mercy. I am hoping that You will always give hope to the hopeless - life to the lifeless and salvation to the lost.

I am filled with the hope of You being You. The King of Kings – The Lord of Lords - The Prince of Peace - The Lily of the Valley - The Root and Offspring of David - The I Am - The Alpha and Omega - The Beginning and the End - The First and the Last - The Son of the Living God - He that was dead and art alive for evermore.

I will not forget You. All my hopes begin and end with You.

Happy New Year to us!

Reflections

_____

_____

YOU GOT LIFE - YOU AIN'T GETTING OUT

A mother wishes that she could gather all of her children under her wings like a mother hen gathers her chicks. She wishes she could make them go into a room and not come out until they have kissed, hugged, and made up. The trouble is they are no longer small children, even though she can't always tell.

Sons – daughters - wives – husbands – daughters-in-laws – nieces – nephews – brothers – sisters – mothers and fathers-in–laws. They don't seem to realize how much the black family of yesterday has brought to the black family of today. We need each other. We are one body with many members. One part cannot function properly without the other.

Try as you may, everyone needs someone for one thing or the other. None of us is an island. We were not designed to cut off people and live in our own self-created world. This world, this family belongs to God, and no one person can have it - control it or destroy it. So, let us try to do better and love better - understand better and forgive better.

You cannot choose to be a part of a family only when you need or want something. A family is 24/7 - no breaks - no holidays - no vacations - no sick time and no I don't want to be bothered today days.

Family is forever. I did not say that family was perfect. It is not by any definition. God created the first family, and it was surely not perfect, so what makes you think yours will be?

Stop always comparing the family that God has given you to everyone elses' perfect family that you know or think you know. No family or family member is perfect, not even you, and most of the time, when we think they are, we are on the outside looking in, and that vantage point always looks better when you don't have to live there.

Appreciate the family God has given to you. He gave it to you for a reason. He put you just where you are supposed to be so stop complaining to everyone else and complain to Him. I am sure He is just waiting to hear your thoughts and opinions about His decision.

Stop trying to get out of it. It won't happen. You got life! There is no getting out so, make it easy on yourself and everyone else. Together we can do this.

Reflections

_____

_____

UNCERTAINTIES

We may not be where we want to be right now at this present moment. Though we have for a time, been removed from our comfort zones by circumstances beyond our control, we are never removed from You.

Your watchful eye is always leading us, and Your Righteous Right Hand always upholds us. So, we go forth in this day knowing that our God is a Mighty God, and You will not fail to show Yourself mighty for us as we face the uncertainties of this day.

Reflections

_____

_____

LIFE SUPPORT

When we hear the words "Life Support," whether they are pertaining to us or someone that we love, fear grips us because we realize that we - they cannot breathe alone and we are in a dangerous situation. No breath - No life.

Little do we realize this simple fact. We are all on Life Support 24/7 - 365 days a year, because if God should ever decide to stop allowing us to breathe His breath (for our breath is not our own). Our Life Support is gone. The plug is pulled. No breath - No life.

Reflections

_____

_____

WHAT IS YOUR NAME AGAIN?

How many times have you run into someone and recognized their face but could not for the life of you remember their name? Were you embarrassed beyond measure? Yes!

God has said that He has engraved our names upon the palms of His hands.

He will never forget your name - your pain - your situation - your prayer - your work - your faith - your health. Anything that pertains to you, He will not forget.

Reflections

_____

_____

STAY WITH ME

No matter where I am

How far I go

In the midst of my going left when You said go right

You know I have no chance to survive out here and finally get to
You

Unless You stay with me

Reflections

_____

_____

JUST FOR ME

If there had been no one else on this entire earth but me, God, You still would have sacrificed Your Son

Just for me

Lord, You still would have gone willingly to the cross, endured the suffering – shame - pain and given your life

Just for me

You still would have shed your blood for the forgiveness of my sins - taken the sting out of death - and declared victory over the grave

Just for me

I thank You, Lord, that even though You would have done it just for me, it was not

Just for me.

Reflections

_____

_____

IT IS NOT ABOUT YOU

There is not one of us that will fail to experience someone we know - we love transition from one state of being to another. To put it more plainly, from life to death

This is never an easy transition, but it is a necessary one. I just want to let you know that certain things happen prior to this transition.

It may seem to you like are being ignored - not loved anymore - shut out because your loved one no longer pays attention to you - responds to you - talks to you -touches you.

Do not take offense

It is not about you.

Maybe all of your life this person made it all about you, not now. Perhaps you are regretting things you said - did or things you failed to do - to say. Regardless...

It is not about you.

You are no longer on their mind once they go to that place where the only one who has access to them is God. There is no longer any room or any need for you. I know this may sound harsh - break your heart and make you want to deny it but this is truth.

They feel no more anger – unforgiveness - disappointment toward you.

It is not about you.

It is about them and their God. The only voice they need or want to hear is the voice of their Redeemer, so as much as you can possibly do before this transition starts to take place, do it.

Listen to your love one - don't shut them off as if what they are saying does not matter – does not make sense to you or because it hurts you to hear it.

It is not about you.

If you have regrets – grudges – unforgiveness - unconfessed sin against them, NOW is the time to talk to them. Don't wait because the time will come when your words – actions - gestures will no longer matter to them.

"Give me my flowers while I am still alive and can smell their fragrance and behold their beauty." That statement's meaning goes far beyond natural flowers. It means tell them you love them often - make a phone call when they are on your mind - stop by and give them a hug - pick up something for them that you know they would like - text them. Do whatever it takes to show your love while they are here because that time of transition comes for all of us. No matter when it comes - how long it takes - what transpires during that time, at that present moment,

It is not about you.

Can you imagine some of the questions people ask in the middle of someone's most precious time alone with their God?

"Is there any insurance, a will? Who is in charge? What did they leave me? What am I going to do? Where will I live?" Wow! Their transition has not even fully taken place, and all you can think about is you.

You should have checked those boxes while it still meant something to your love one because right now, at this present moment in time, they do not care and as hard as it might be for you to accept

It is not about you.

Reflections

PAY YOUR VOWS UNTO THE LORD

Judges 11:29 begins to tell the story of Jephthah as he was making a vow to the Lord (not a deal), saying that if the Ammonites were given into his hands, whatever was the first thing that came out of his door when he returned home in triumph to meet him would be sacrificed to the Lord for a burnt offering.

He returned victoriously but guess what? The first thing that came out of his door to meet him dancing to the sounds of the timbrels was his daughter - his only child. He tore his clothes in mourning and devastation because he had made a vow to the Lord that he could not break. His daughter understood and prepared herself to be a willing sacrifice. After two months of preparation, she returned to her father, and he did to her as he had vowed.

Beware of the things your lips utter before the Lord God, for He will not hold you blameless and unaccountable for what you have vowed unto Him. It is better not to make a vow to the Lord than to make it and take it back.

Do not get caught up in moments of intense sorrow or elated happiness. Put your hand over your mouth and endure the sorrow until it has passed. Enjoy the happiness as long as it continues.

Do not make a vow that you cannot or will not keep. Our God does not make deals, and every vow made to Him will be collected.

Reflections

IT IS FINISHED

The blood has been shed

The debt has been paid

The job has been finished

The sacrifice is complete

He has taken our place

Give thanks for the cross

And especially for the cross bearer

The risen Jesus Christ our Lord and Saviour

For had He not risen, the cross his place of death,

would have been of no avail and our faith would be in vain

HAPPY RESURRECTION DAY

Reflections

_____

_____

NEVER FORGETTING

Never forgetting that whose I am makes me who I am

I am a child of not just a king but "The King" and I forever eat at the Kings' table

Don't ever let anyone forget whose you are. Don't ever let anyone treat you less than a child of "The King"

Don't you ever forget who and whose you are

Reflections

_____

_____

ALL I HAVE

All I have is because of You

I have all that I need because I have You

Because of You, I have no want

Reflections

_____

_____

NOT THE BEST DAY

Today is not the best day. Do you ever have those days when you don't want to do anything, but you feel like you should be up and doing something?

These are things that no one but you would ever know whether you did or not. Important? Not important? Slept late - need to wash those dishes you left in the sink - clean out the closet - wipe down the walls. Who is going to know but you? Yet, that desire to always please someone else is constantly with you. The sad thing is no one is there - no one sees - no one comes - no one cares.

It is only important to you, so take it off the top of your list. You are okay, and Jesus does not mind. He will sit with you on that couch that is full of unfolded clothes - see past your messy hair –kids needing a bath - your house torn up, and the fact that you are still in your pj's at 3 pm and not say a word.

Maybe your not-the-best-day turned into a great day because you got to sit with your Lord in the midst of your mess, and finally, you never felt the need to please anyone or to explain something that never really needed explaining.

Reflections

_____

_____

JESUS

You are forever waiting, seated at the right hand of God the Father, for that next call of Your name. You're waiting to hear that voice - the voice of one more person that has come to the realization that they can't do it on their own anymore, not that they were able to do it before, but that they need You, for only You can deliver them.

Thank You for those that have already cried out your name. Thank You for the ones that are not yet there but are coming crying out Your name. JESUS.

Reflections

_____

_____

ALL

God is in all places at all times

Reflections

_____

_____

UNEXPECTED DEVASTATION

There are all kinds of situations and circumstances that make us pray in our cars – bathrooms – bedrooms - closets- on our jobs - standing in a line or walking down the street. Oh! But sometimes there are things in life that hit us so unexpectedly and with such force that they almost destroy us, and it seems that none of those previously prayed prayers will do.

Life has literally brought you to your knees and before your Fathers' throne. Try as you might; you cannot get up. You must stay there before the throne. You must stay before Jehovah Jireh, the one that will provide what you seek and what you need. You know without a doubt that you can't handle it. You have to give it to the only One that has all power in His hands. You must trust and depend on Him.

Reflections

_____

_____

CHOOSE

I love you

There are no buts

I only choose to not chase after people who do not want to be caught

I choose not to bother people who show me they do not want to be bothered

I love you - I just choose

Reflections

_____

_____

LONELINESS

When you are a child, young - carefree and doing all the things children do, loneliness has no meaning - no definition for you. Even when playing alone for a while, your mind enjoys the task at hand as you wait with anticipation for someone else to come and join in the game.

HIGH SCHOOL AND COLLEGE - With so much to do, who has time to be lonely? So many friends – parties – pledges – sports - midterms – romances – etc.

Loneliness has no place here.

GRADUATION - There is too much to do. We have to find a job - shop for new clothes - pound the streets trying to find some place to live that we can actually afford. Too much to do.

Loneliness has no place here.

GOT THAT JOB - We are making that money. I am putting in long hours, not a moment to myself. I am busy – busy - busy.

Loneliness has no place here.

FOUND SOMEONE - I am in love. There is so much that goes into the planning of this wedding. If I thought I could not take a moment to catch my breath before...look at me now. I can't stop- have to get it done. Lonely, who? Too involved for that.

Loneliness has no place here.

WE'RE PREGNANT!! - Here come the children - no breaks. It is from one thing to the other 24/7 and 365 days a year. There are no days off from parenthood. Don't forget you still have to work on being that great spouse and supporter, too.

Loneliness has no place here.

EMPTY NEST SYNDROME THEY ARE GONE – They have their new lives in new cities - new families - new jobs - new friends, and they don't always include you.

Maybe you are feeling a little awkward now. Maybe useless is more of a correct word, even though it sounds rather harsh. No worries, you still have your spouse, and you try to stay as active and involved with life as you can.

Loneliness has no place here.

My condolences on the death of your spouse. I know your home on some days just seems like a house with no laughter - no voices - no pressures - no children running around playing or giggling.

Is this you, loneliness? You and I have never met before, and I hoped we never would. You are not my friend, and I am surely not yours. Yet, you always seem to hang around when I look at the phone, waiting for it to ring and it doesn't, or whenever I hope to hear a knock on my door, but it does not come. You are always lurking around at the loneliest part of my day, bedtime. That is when I truly realize how empty this house is, and wished that I had someone to share my end-of-the-day stories - someone to share my bed and keep me warm – someone to get the Ben Gay and rub me.

Loneliness just stands there at every turn wanting nothing more than to move in with me. Sorry, loneliness, I don't like you - don't want you.

You see God has something better planned for me than you. He has replaced you with His all-knowing - all-caring love and comfort, and as I have told you so many times before,

"You, loneliness, have no place here."

"Goodbye."

Reflections

_____

_____

SHE KEEPS HER PLACE

As I was going into my room to talk to God about a tantrum I threw yesterday about what I cannot truly remember. All I can remember was that it was about my typing mistakes and so many do-overs that were taking me off my game -   that I was allowing to take me off my game, and a bunch of other stuff that meant absolutely nothing and in no way was worth it. Is it ever?

Well, anyway, it was 3:10 am, and as I was sitting on the floor, I glanced at the blinds and saw a light. I first thought it was the lamp post, but on second glance, it was too high. It was the moon.

I don't know how long it had been since I had actually intentionally taken time to look, not glance, at the moon. It looked so amazingly beautiful to me that I turned off my house alarm - grabbed my robe - a blanket - a box of tissues - my cup of tea, and ventured onto my balcony to see one of God's creations that I had taken for granted.

Well, once I got settled, my observation of her began. There were no stars that I could see, and some of the sky seemed clear, but where she stood, clouds surrounded her. They were all shapes and sizes, and some of them had faces like we have all imagined them having at one time or another.

I was confused at first because the clouds looked like they were taking her out, overshadowing her and forcing her to move from her rightful place. That is where God had placed her. She belonged there. When I really took the time to look, the clouds were behind her at all times. She was so bright that the darkness of the clouds behind her sometimes made her appear to be somewhat dim, and I thought she was running from them, but as I looked more intensely, they were moving slowly past her from behind. They were getting out of her way. She never moved - never yielded any of her brightness or her God-given glory.

She stood her ground even though some of the clouds, I would venture to say, were evil-looking and looked as if they could swallow her whole; they passed by. When you next saw them, they were to the east of her and looked like nothing more than a pillow you could lie your head upon.

I can imagine God putting her there and decreeing that she not move for anything. She was in her place - she belonged there, and all that tried to move her and snuff out her brilliant light that gave light to the darkness, well, maybe they belonged there too, but only for a reason - only for a season.

The reason being that she would forever know that nothing can move her from where God and God alone has destined she be. Well, we all know that seasons are only for a while.

When I went and looked an hour later, she was standing all alone. There were no clouds taking away from her God given glory. She stood alone. So, stand moon and let your light always shine to show the way to us who are wandering in the darkness. The ones that need to be reminded of our steadfastness to never be moved by people - circumstances or transitions that enter our lives for a reason or a season.

Remind us that we are who and what God says we are, and we will hold our places of destiny as you hold yours. God has put us here in this place.

Reflections

_____

_____

FRIEND

There was never any other face that I saw when the word friend was mentioned other than yours. No other face - ever.

I would have given my life for you, my friend, and I did. I thought and believed with all I had inside of me that you would, without question, do the same. I was wrong, though. The friend I loved with all my heart did not love me - did not look out for me - did not protect me - did not fight for me or with me. They did not possess the love that was equal to mine.

When? When did your love for me and your loyalty to me change? Did I feel it - know it, and just let it pass? Was I once again overthinking or tripping about something that would end up, as always, no big deal?

What could anyone have said to you about me? Me, your friend, your best friend? What could they have whispered in your ear or put in your spirit about me, your friend, that could have changed your love for me into hate?

If I had not been there - seen it - felt it - lived it and died it, I never would have believed what has now become known as the truth.

You may not have known this then, but I want you to know it now. In the last moments - hours of my life, my mind was on you - my eyes were on you - my heart was on you, and even if you could not or chose not to hear it, I was asking, "Why, why? What did I do to you that would allow you to stand idly by and, by your complacency, give your permission to others to assault me while you just watched me, your friend, die in front of your eyes?"

Your face, my friend, even with my eyes closed, was the last I saw, and I hope mine was the last you saw before I left you and Jesus came and took me home.

Listen when your parents tell you that someone is no good for you. They have more experience than you think. Pick your friends carefully, my friends. Too many people have ended up like me. I thought I knew what a real friend was, but, in the end, I didn't. I wish I could tell you to be aware of red flags. Trust that people are who they show themselves to be. When you feel it is time to part, don't let anyone including yourself, especially yourself, talk you out of it. Feelings – inklings - warnings are real. TAKE HEED!

Reflections

_____

_____

ONLY TEARS

I don't want to talk about it

I don't even want to think about it

There are no answers

Only tears

My mouth can't seem to form the words

My voice refuses to be heard

Only tears

So much going on inside

Locked up - shut up and can't get out

Only tears

Even though there is no sound,

Everything inside is overwhelming and loud

Only tears

Please hear what my tears are trying to say to you

Reflections

_____

_____

THE MAN IN THE WINDOW

I had just gotten off the subway on my way home from work. I was enjoying the sounds of the city that never seemed to sleep. As I passed by this apartment building, I just happened to look up into the windows. Some had blinds that were open. Some had blinds that are closed. Some don't have any blinds at all.

My eyes stopped on the window with the man on the exercise bike. For some reason, it just looked like he was in a world of his own, a world that he was not comfortable with, a world that he wanted to change, but for who and why.

"Peddle, peddle, peddle, go, go, go", the words seemed to be flying out of the window into the atmosphere. He had worked hard all day, and now he was at it again, but where was she? Where was the person that he was doing all this for? She should have been home by now. He was waiting to see the joy on her face when she opened the door and saw that he was trying to be all that she wanted and thought he should be. He only wanted to make her proud, to make her love him like he loved her.

It had been over an hour now, and she had not come through the door.

As he slowly and reluctantly got off the bike, the phone rang, and he answered it. It was her, and she said something had come up at the office and she would be there later. His heart and head dropped. "Can't you come right away?" "I said I will be there when I get there.", and from the sound of her voice, he knew it was not going to be a good evening when she got there.

His body began to tense up in preparation for what he knew would happen. He made sure all things were in their places, for the time being at least. The bike, should he put it away or leave it out? Leave it out. Maybe if she saw he was trying, things would not get too out of hand - maybe.

It is right after 11:00 PM, and her key is now opening the door. "Hey baby," he said as he went to hug her and help her out of her coat, but no, she was having no part of that, no part of him. She brushed past him so hard and fast that she almost knocked him over. "Dinner's ready, babe and I was working out on the bike like you wanted me to, but you took so long getting home you didn't see me. Do you want me to show you how far I got before dinner?" "First of all, you don't question me about how late I get in. You better be glad I even come here at all, and the bike, that's a laugh. Can you even fit it? I didn't think they made one large enough for a whale. It would take two bikes to even begin to help you, and how long do you really expect me, looking like I do, to wait for you to look decent enough to be seen in public with me?" She laughed uncontrollably and hatefully.

He seemed to just shrink at her words. They were so hurtful, and he was trying all he knew to make her happy with him. It just wasn't enough for her. Nothing he did or gave her seemed to be. He had an excellent job paying six figures plus bonuses. She wore the best of clothes and jewelry in the tens of thousands. He withheld no material wealth from her. She wanted it - he got it, no questions asked, because if he didn't, every encounter would turn into what this night was about to become.

As he went to take the dinner out of the oven, she went into a rage knocking the dishes with the food on them to the floor. Pieces of glass popped up and hit him right under his right eye, and it was bleeding profusely, but he didn't have time now to attend to it. He was too busy warding off her kicks - punches and dodging forks, glasses and anything else she could throw, not just throw but make contact. He slowly tried to get closer to her so maybe he could get behind her and put his arms around her to make her stop - cool down - quit! It wasn't happening with her. She was in a rage, and there never had to be a reason for it. It was just whenever she felt like it. She hurled all kinds of insults at him. Every derogatory word she could think of to say, she said, killing him more with her words aimed at his spirit than the actual tangible thing she threw at him. They were things that cut – bruised - broke ribs - busted lips and bloodied noses.

He finally could ward her off of him and, in tears and sobs, ran to

152

his safe room, the one room that she could not get into to hurt him anymore. He loved her; there was no doubt about that, but right now, she was raging, and he needed the protection this room provided.

How many times will he go through this? He didn't want to hurt her - did not want to call the police - did not want to be embarrassed and ashamed. This time was really bad, and he already knew work was out of the question for at least three days. He could barely move, much less work.

Outside the door, she was still at it, daring him to come out and fight like a man instead of running like a punk. That went on for hours, and she finally stopped. Sometime during the night and between all sorts of plans he could devise in his mind, as he had so often done, sleep found him, and he rested, and for a while, he found some peace and laid all of himself into that peace.

When he finally awakened, the apartment was quiet. It was around 9:00 AM. Was it a trick to get him to come out and risk another attack, or had she really left and gone to work like nothing at all had happened like she so often did? Well, he needed to relieve himself, so he had to see. He slowly opened the door and looked out. Well, for sure, the house was still trashed. He ventured cautiously out into the apartment and looked in their bedroom. She was gone just like that. No words - no "I'm sorry" - no angry commands, demanding him to have this apartment cleaned up by the time she got home. Nothing. Just gone.

153

He breathed a sigh of relief as deep as he could with what he thought were bruised ribs. He had a cut eye - scratched face, neck and arms - knot on his forehead from a bottle that was thrown, maybe even a broken nose. He thought about putting on his clothes, hat and shades and going to the emergency room. He had thought about it many times before but never did

Last night was really bad, and he decided to put shame - embarrassment, and pride behind him and go get himself some medical attention. He left. He took the subway to get the help that he so desperately needed. He looked as if he had been beaten and mugged, so they took him back right away. There were so many questions he almost left, but he didn't. He told of all the domestic violence he had suffered for years at the hands of his wife. It was scary, but he was more tired of it happening than he was scared of sharing it.

He was treated and admitted for a few days, and in the meantime, his wife was served and arrested for domestic violence. She was adamant and enraged by his non true accusation of abuse. When he left the hospital, a temporary restraining order (TRO) was already in place against his wife, and she could come no closer than within 500 feet of him at any given time. He cleaned the apartment of what he wanted, cleared out his bank account of all that belonged to him, and he left that city that never sleeps and that woman he could never satisfy no matter how hard he tried. He left, and he never turned around. He never looked back.

Try to remember that women are not the only people being abused. They are sometimes the abusers. Abuse is not OK, no matter who the abuser is.

Reflections

_____

_____

YOUR FACE

As much as you may try,

Your face will never hide

How you really feel

Reflections

_____

_____

PAIN

We hear over and over again that there is no pain that God cannot feel, and when we are going through difficult- extremely unbearable pain, we need - we want those words to apply to us like they never have before.

Someone may have left us in so much pain - feeling so much hurt that we don't believe God can feel this much pain or that this pain can touch Him at all. Our pain is very real to us, and no one feels it or knows it like we do.

On the other hand, how many people have we left hurt in pain? How many families have we destroyed with our mouth - actions that cannot be taken back? Sometimes never giving a second glance or thought of the wreckage we have left behind as we try to concentrate and move past our own pain. It doesn't feel too good to be reminded of that face we have tried to forget - that situation we chose to ignore when we could have helped - that action we took that was so totally unnecessary and did so much damage.

God will not let us forget until we repent. Ask forgiveness from God first, and if possible, from the person we hurt and caused so much pain.

God does feel our pain, but He also feels the pain of the people left behind in the aftermath of our yester life.

Take a minute, breathe, and let us remember the pain someone has caused us and forgive them as we have asked to be forgiven for the pain, we, too,have caused.

God is no respecter of persons. He forgives because He feels all pain - not just ours - everyone's.

Reflections

VISIBLE VS. INVISIBLE

Am I only visible to you when my answers are yes to any request, demand or order that you give me? It has been going on for so very long that I guess I had accepted it as the norm - the abuse that my mind has endured all of these years. What happened to me? Where did I go?

"Do this- do that - dress like this - show up with a smile on your face- act like you love me - like you care - make someone believe that I care about you - convince them that I am all of this person they think I am - do your job." That is all you ever say to me.

Being visible is not all it is cracked up to be when the only time you see me is when you need me to make you more visible (as if you needed any help with that) or to make your lies more believable.

Unless I am needed for something, I am more invisible than The Invisible Man. Invisibility gets me no "Good mornings" from you - no concerns from you pertaining to my mental or physical state and without question, no concern for my spiritual condition.

We are just two people passing through the same house, not home day after day - night after night over and over again for more years than I should have ever allowed.

I gave you the power to make me invisible early in our relationship, trying to please you, trying to be what you wanted me to be. I was living by your rules and having no power to make any rules of my own. I was constantly making myself smaller and smaller and of no value while letting your ego continue to grow.

Even though I worked and was a professional just like you, every penny I made went to you, with you giving me what you thought I should have. No question you were the boss, the smarter one, you said. You sure can't prove that to me now, but for so many years, you made me question my worth - my intelligence - my beauty - the love of my family. The emotional and financial abuse I suffered under the one that was supposed to be my covering - my protector almost destroyed me. You were the husband that was supposed to love me like Christ loved the church - that vowed before God to love - honor and cherish me. You didn't.

There are a lot of things I could call you, but the head of the house would not be one because you never followed Christ, yet I followed you for so long, putting on facades in Gods' house - smiling on the outside while on the inside, I knew you did not live a word you spoke and you even had the audacity to teach others how to treat their wives when you had not opened your mouth to your own wife in 67days and sometimes longer. I got the receipts.

I also share some of the blame if I am at fault for honoring my vows when friends and family said I should have been long gone. What can I say? After all of these years, I find myself in the same place.

The only difference being that I am now completely comfortable with my invisibility to you. I no longer desire to be visible to you. I am totally visible to myself, and I love what I see in me, and I also realize that you are and were whom you had always been. I guess with all of the invisibility that had been going on, so much of you had been invisible to me, too, - not anymore. I see all of you, and I am just happy to be free of any control you once had over me.

Sincerely,

Wife in Name Only

Reflections

_____

_____

YOU WONDER

We care about our children even with all the things they have done. People wonder why wonder we care. We should have given up on them by now with all the home training we have given – tears we have cried - prayers we have prayed – hurts we have endured - sleepless nights that have come and gone - stories we have heard, and things we have seen.

Yet, we do not give up; we keep fighting, not that natural fight but a spiritual fight because we know and we believe our weapons are not carnal, but mighty through God to the pulling down of strongholds. God makes all the difference because with Him and through Him, all things are possible. So, our fight does not stop where yours does.

Because they are not your children and you are not in this position, you can say, "Give up. Let them go." We, too, give up and let them go. We just do not give them over to the enemy–the destroyer, the deceiver. We give them over to God. They belong to Him, and He is quite capable of handling them even in the darkest of situations where we can see no light. God is light - God is love.

Where would we have been, yes, you and me, if God had given up on us and not loved us enough to send His only Son to deliver us from the enemy and save us? Where?

We stand strong with our Mighty God, and we call all things that be not as though they were. We are going to wait, for in the end, we shall see God's glory in their lives.

Reflections

_____

_____

HURT PEOPLE

Hurt people hurt people

Hurt people also draw other hurt people to them

Hurt people can become healed people

Were you ever hurt, but now you are healed?

Reflections

_____

_____

SUNDAY MORNING CHURCH

Some days, but mostly Sundays, Murphy's Law wants to rule but

Thank God that God's Law always overrules

I know this because I made it

I am here in this place today

Reflections

_____

_____

FATHERS

No matter what kind of father you perceive yourself to be, God can always see another, and his perception is, without a doubt, always right

You may have always been that father that worked day and night for his children and made sure they had everything and anything they wanted or needed except you - your love - your time

Maybe you were/are

A trying to be a father - not knowing how because you never had a father to teach you

A scared father - so afraid of messing up that you decided running off and leaving was the best thing you could do

A macho father - only showing your son the way to be a man was by violence and taking what you want - never telling him itwas OK to hurt - to cry - to be afraid - to ask for help

A never wanted to be a father - but found yourself being one anyway

A trying so hard to become a father

A tired of all the wrong choices I have made, father

Abused as a child father

CEO of a company father

THIS ONE'S JUST 4 U

Pastor father

Drug Lord father

Wanting to be the perfect father

Not trusting myself to be a father, father

A child who hates me, father

An I don't know how to be a better father, father

I need someone to teach me, father

Never let the people see the real me, father

A dress to the Tee - never a hair out of place - money in my pocket - women on my side, father

Whoever you are - wherever you find yourself on this list, God saw you first, and you or your situation is never too big for Him

Give Him all you can't handle - can't fix, and He will willingly do it for you. He knows it all. He feels what you feel, and He calls you to come to your Father, the One that will teach you all you ever need to know about being a father

God loves you - God knows you - God celebrates you for doing all you know how to do

Now let him do what only He knows how to do

Reflections

MESS - UPS

Mess -ups? I think that my name is attached to far more than I care to admit.

Some days the bad outweighs the good - the dont's outweigh the do's, or the do's outweigh the dont's; it depends on the direction the mess - up is taking.

But you know what? Just like a mother or father who has seen what a mess you have made and hear that "I'm sorry" coming from your mouth, they clean it up so well you can hardly see the mess you KNOW you had made.

Our father sees the "I'm sorry", coming from our hearts, and He cleans not only the mess we have made to the point of it no longer being seen - that is not enough for Him. He does not stop there; He also cleans up the messer-upper -me and you.

Reflections

_____

_____

"HOW ARE YOU?"

Everyday questions with everyday answers "I'm good." "Blessed." "I'm fine." How many times have you heard those replies or given them as your own? Are you really - are we really?

We are just thankful that most people can't see through the lies we tell. Are they really lies, or is it calling things that be not as though they were? A combination of both, I dare to say, because, on most days, we are hoping and praying that the answer to these questions that we give would be true.

Facades, most of us wear them 14 to 15 hours a day, allotting for sleep and only sleep to know the real us. Even with the people closest to us, I mean people we live with - sleep with - see on a daily basis, and work with. They don't know us completely; we have not shared all of our fears - inadequacies or real truths with them. We have told no one. We even try not to tell God but He already knows.

People that we meet just by chance in the line at the grocery store - doctor's office - mall or restaurant, we are more open with them in a two to ten-minute conversation than we are with the people we know. Why? Why would that be? Maybe because you will never cross paths with them again - because they don't even know your name - because they have no expectations of you - because you know they could really care less, and you just needed to tell someone. Strangers make good sounding boards.

Can we really trust the people we live our everyday lives with with the truth about ourselves? Do they really want to know? Will it change their opinion or perception of us? Will they withdraw the love they have given us, the love we are accustomed to having?

Perhaps you tried in the past to share, and you came away from that attempt feeling totally and utterly crushed - defeated and sick with sorrow because you willingly dared to be vulnerable, and that response was one you never want to experience again.

I will not tell you that there is no one to whom you can share your truth. There is someone somewhere. I will tell you though, that you definitely have a friend in Jesus. There is nothing about you - your life - your past that He can't handle hearing - nothing that will change His opinion or perception of you. There is nothing that will ever cause Him to withhold His love from you. Why? Because He already knows, and He still loves you. Talk to Him. You can trust Him.

Reflections

_____

_____

HEY, MOM

I know you have sacrificed a lot for me, even taking from yourself to make sure I was "straight." Sometimes I may seem ungrateful and unappreciative, but I'm not. I get in my feelings and feel some kind of way sometimes, but I know I would be totally lost without you in my corner.

Just hang in there with me, please, for just a little while longer. I'm growing up, and you will see that I'm worth it.

What can I say, I came from you, and you were - are and always will definitely be worth it. Just wait! Don't give up on me! I will make you proud to call me son/daughter.

Reflections

_____

_____

DAYS

There are days you get tired

Days that it takes a lot to do all the things you do

Days when you feel like you just don't have the strength to do it
again

Days that you feel unappreciated and overlooked

Days when you wonder if you have really done the best you could
do or even what was expected of you

Don't get weary - God sees you - Don't doubt - He loves you

He will strengthen you one day at a time

Keep doing what you do

Reflections

_____

_____

JUST DO IT

We're just so accustomed to speaking to Siri - Alexa and whomever else we call when we want an instant response - answer that we hardly do anything manually anymore.

Why not let our fingers gently move over the pages of Esther - I and II Chronicles – Joel – Matthew - I and II Kings - James etc.? Put those readers on - adjust them - clean them if you must and just do it. Read those stories that you had forgotten about but now seem to be springing up to life in your soul.

I would venture to guess that you are actually enjoying the Word and the questions coming to your mind. The Holy Spirit is giving you so many answers.

You have almost forgotten that lunchtime has passed. You have been feeding on the word for over 2 hours. Guess what? No one has called your name, and if they did, you did not hear them or better yet, you chose to ignore them. The house did not catch on fire, and your soul feels so good. No more excuses. Just do it.

Those friends you can't seem to go five minutes without talking to, texting or emailing have not even called you, and you totally forgot about that picture on television you just could not miss watching. You forgot all about them - about it. You remembered God.

Just do it, my brother and my sister and see how easy it becomes for you to let everyone and everything go, and go to God.

Just do it, now.

Reflections

_____

_____

FATHER VS DADDY

I looked up the difference between a father and a daddy. A father is someone who contributes to the physical creation of a child from whom the sperm has been obtained to fertilize the mother's ovum. A daddy gives guidance and love to his children, in addition to supplying them with the necessities in life.

Men, as you read this, in what category do you find yourself? More importantly, if your child is reading this be they young or old, in what category do they find you?

If you find yourself to be a daddy, kudos to you and much love. Keep it up!

If you find yourself to be a father, it is not too late to switch sides - to want to do better - to attempt to do better. You can have that hard conversation and ask for forgiveness. You can have a second or even a tenth chance. It's up to you. The ball is in your court. Don't stop. Your children need you.

Reflections

_____

_____

HOT SHOWER

I sometimes compare sin to a hot shower. When you just get into it, it is so hot you want to jump out, but the longer it runs, the more comfortable it becomes, and now you want to turn it up until it is as hot as it can get.

You didn't even realize until you got out that you were burnt and in need of a balm for your healing.

Reflections

_____

_____

GOD SAYS

Seek My Face

Acknowledge Me in All That You Do

Carry Yourself in a Way That Bringeth Honor to My Name

Reflections

_____

_____

HOW?

What can be troubling you? You look like you just stepped off the cover of a fashion magazine.

God sees your tears. Tears that you shed in the middle of the night, wondering- wondering how long you can make this work - how long you can keep up this charade - how long you can keep being- doing what you really never wanted to be or do. Maybe you did at one time, but that time has long passed.

You're in too deep - too many folks looking up to you - looking for you to feed them from a table that you no longer wish to sit. How do you do it? How do you get out?

You're surrounded by smiling faces, but not all of those faces are loyal to you. They can't even see the tears your eyes are trying to hold back - the tiredness in your eyes - your voice - your posture. They think you just need a little rest, and for sure, you do. They just don't understand that the rest you seek - you need cannot come from a vacay or a few days of good sleep.

You need to get out- out of this crazy life- dangerous life- thieving life - wheeling and dealing life - truthless life - this by any means necessary life.

You need to get out. And you know this because, for a long time now, you have heard that voice within yourself telling you "No" when you want to do wrong. You never really heard that before, or your heart was too hard to hear it then. You hear it more and more now in every act you make- step you take- plan you make. You can't get away from it. You put your hands over your ears, but it's useless, the voice continues. In the quietness of the day or night, whenever you get a moment alone- a moment to be still, the tears come like a rain that can't be stopped, and the voice you hear tells you that this is no longer the place you belong. It never was. You have another place to be - another life to live - another kind of table to sit at, another kind of people to feed. You hear it - You know it - you believe it. You just don't know how to do it. "How do I exit? How do I leave? How do I walk away? How do I leave the only life I've ever known for a life I know nothing about?"

This writer says, "I don't know". What I do know is that with God, all things are possible and that if He's telling you to do it, He will make the way. His plan, his purpose for your life, will not be thwarted, it will not be stopped. He knows the plans he has for you - Plans to prosper you - not to harm you. Plans to give you a future and a hope.

How many times has He saved your life- how many times has he offered you an easy way out? You never took it. Now, you find yourself in the hardest place in life you have ever been. He will allow whatever he has to allow to save your life but rest assured that your faith – hope - belief in God and His voice will be rewarded, and He will never fail you. He has and always will have complete power over everything and everyone. He is omnipotent. His grace awaits you. Go to him as a son goes to a father (even if you have never had that kind of relationship with your natural father, I know you have imagined many times what that might feel like.) Submit your all to Him. Give Him your heart - your love - your sins - your fears. He already knows you. He knows all you are and all you are not. Your struggles and your dreams are not hidden from Him, He has just been waiting for you to come. He will lead you from here. God bless you in your new place - your new life, Kingdom Leader. Wherever it may take you, God will be there.

Reflections

_____

_____

FOR YOU

I want and need you to forgive me but

If you never forgive me for me, please forgive me for you

Unforgiveness is a heavy burden that keeps us in bondage

Free yourself, if not for me, for you

Reflections

_____

_____

NOT FORGOTTEN

I don't have to be the center of your life

I don't even have to be relevant in your everyday life

I only want not to be forgotten

Reflections

_____

_____

"STEPPIN"

This is a new day

Forgetting old things- remembering them no more

I am stepping forward into this new day and all the possibilities it
holds

Here I come

Reflections

_____

_____

MAYBE

"What's wrong? What's the matter?" These are the questions that we constantly ask each other. We want answers, no doubt about that. We know there is something wrong. We just can't figure out what exactly it is.

Maybe we do know, and we just don't want to say it out loud.

Maybe we know it's over.

Maybe we know the love is gone.

Maybe we know we have hurt long enough.

Maybe we are just tired.

Maybe we just don't know what else to do.

Maybe we have just lost each other in the busyness of what we call life.

Maybe we haven't tried to fix this.

Maybe we have given up too soon.

Maybe we have forgotten the vows that we made to each other before God.

Maybe we can still make this work if we put each other first again and let everyone and everything else get in line.

Maybe we stopped praying - stop trusting God and tried to fix things ourselves, and they just got worse.

I don't know which maybe is true.

Maybe they all are.

Maybe we can start today asking God for His help in renewing and restoring the love we first had.

He won't have a "maybe" answer for us, He will have a "Yes, I will help you, Just been waiting for you to ask" answer.

Reflections

_____

_____

REAL

The struggle is real

God is realeerrrrr!

Reflections

About the Author

Sharon Barbee Simmons resides in Charlotte, NC, where she is an active member of the Macedonia Church of Charlotte, a woman of God, and Mother of Zion.

She was married to the late William Simmons and is the proud mother and grandmother of a blended family that consists of 8 children and 17 grandchildren.

Sharon started journaling decades ago in an attempt to express her feelings on paper. Later, she began writing letters to God about the things she faced—struggled with, overcame, and is still finding herself faced with daily.

She continued writing because she realized that with the urging of the Holy Spirit, she was able to express herself more openly and truthfully with the written word than a spoken word, enabling her to make more of an impact on the lives of people.

Made in the USA
Columbia, SC
06 May 2024

35338130R00104